ERMINE TALES

Also by the Earl of Carnarvon:

NO REGRETS

ERMINE TALES

❋

The Earl of Carnarvon

Ode To All Men

A man is not old when his hair grows grey,
A man is not old when his teeth decay,
But a man must prepare for his last long sleep
When his mind makes a date that his body can't keep.

Weidenfeld and Nicolson
London

Contents

The author and publishers are grateful to the following sources for kind permission to reproduce illustrations: Radio Times Hulton Picture Library, 3, 4; Sport and General Press Agency, 5, 8; Keystone Press Agency, 9; Mr Day, 12; Ministry of Agriculture, Fisheries and Food (Crown Copyright), 14. All other photographs are from the author's collection.

Illustrations

Preface

I HAVE HAD numerous letters from people all over the world who have read *No Regrets* asking me to write some more anecdotes. I am flattered beyond belief that so many had such fun reading it. I love giving pleasure whenever I can.

I have called this book *Ermine Tales* for on the few occasions when I have opened Highclere, my Hampshire home, for charitable purposes I have always been surprised to notice that the many visitors who pour through the library, instead of gazing at the glorious Romney over the fireplace, invariably make a bee-line for a somewhat faded photograph of me in my coronation robes of ermine and velvet. It seems to fascinate them, so I hope you will be equally amused by these stories and find that there is something here for everybody's taste.

This will certainly be – this I guarantee – my very last shot at trying to portray, to those of you who are interested, life as it was lived between 1900 and the present day. As far as the feudal system is concerned, I am indeed one of the last.

Had I not been lucky enough to have enjoyed the help and advice of three fervent fans of NO REGRETS, *Venetia, Betty and 'Puff', who continually encouraged me to complete this labour of love, I know full well it would have been stillborn — many will think, and some will say, that this would have been the best result! I hope that others will differ and be amused by my tales, which are all factual and quite true.*

To the devoted trio who have guided me I tender my most grateful thanks.

1
The Stately Home

I HAVE ALWAYS loved Highclere, and have spent the
happiest years of my life under its roofs. My great-
grandfather, the third Earl of Carnarvon, altered and
reconstructed the original eighteenth-century house,
turning it into the great castle it is today. A sportsman,
an excellent shot and a lover of hunting, he knew the
countryside for miles around. He wished to enhance
both the house and the land and he spared no expense in
so doing.

His son, my grandfather, was of a more serious turn
of mind, a scholar and a keen politician, he was frequently abroad in the Queen's service. He held the
position of Colonial Secretary and later was appointed
Viceroy of Ireland. Despite his foreign travels, he spent
a great deal of time embellishing Highclere and took a
great interest in farming.

He hated racing but enjoyed the breeding of live-
stock, his particular hobby was the raising of Berkshire
pigs, of which he had a very good herd. He named one
of his best boars Ormonde, which was also the name of
a well-known racehorse.

On Derby Day, he returned from London to Highclere on the afternoon train and, as usual, the station-

master, wearing his top hat and full regalia, met him coming off the train and escorted him to his carriage. To make conversation, the stationmaster said, 'I've good news for you m'lord, you'll be pleased to hear that Ormonde won today.'

'Good,' said my grandfather, 'I always thought very highly of him. Mind you, that was only the Bath and West. Now you have told me this, I shall not be surprised if he wins at the Royal.'

There is a tale told about a gardener who worked here in my father's time. He came from an old Hampshire family and his name was William Stickers. He had never left Highclere but his friends told him that he and his wife ought to see London.

One day they made their way to Newbury, driven in a pony trap by one of their friends. When they reached Newbury Station, he saw them safely on to the train.

On their arrival at Paddington, the first thing that met their eyes was 'Billstickers will be Prosecuted'.

That was enough for him!

'I ain't goin' no further,' he said, 'that's a warning, Mary. We be goin' back on very next train we can get.'

I think this is a charming little story and it may well be the case that those who lived in the serenity of the countryside enjoyed a happier life than those of us who are continually on the move.

Another old gardener who worked on the estate here for many years revelled in the name of Digweed.

Mr Digweed had a daughter called Daisy and one day she arrived at Highclere School looking very scruffy, badly dressed and with a pungent body odour. The headmistress wrote a note to her mother which read as follows: 'Dear Mrs Digweed, Unless Daisy returns tomorrow well scrubbed and neatly dressed, I regret to tell you that I shall not be able to continue having her here as a pupil.'

The following day, Daisy returned properly groomed and presented this note to the headmistress: 'Dear Headmistress, We knows our Dysy aint no rose but we sent her to school to be learnt, not smelt!'

My dear father loved Highclere but he was lazy by nature. He was only too delighted to see improvements made as long as he did not have to pay for them. So he was very pleased when, in 1911, my mother arranged to have electricity installed in the castle and the bill was paid for by her father, Alfred de Rothschild.

My father was not so pleased when income tax went up from sixpence to ninepence. Such was his fury that we nearly had a day of mourning. Dead silence all through lunch and only an odd grunt when we assembled for the evening meal.

In my father's day there were about twenty-six indoor servants as well as a permanent night-watchman and I'm not counting the stable and outdoor staff. There was of course no central heating and no running water so that there were innumerable fires to be cleaned out and re-laid daily and hot water had to be carried upstairs to all the bedrooms. When visitors came they would bring their own personal servants with them to add to the throng, a man would have his valet and his wife would have her own personal maid who looked after her clothes and jewellery and helped her to dress. During the shooting season guests might also bring their own loaders. At the end of a long rainy day there would be guns to be cleaned, wet clothes to be dried, dogs to be fed and kennelled. A great many extra people would need attention indoors and out.

My mother had her own groom of the chambers, a very good-looking man called Roberts. His job was to see to my mother's comfort. For example, he would arrange that she had writing paper and pens in her boudoir. When she travelled he made sure there were cushions at her back and a rug to keep her warm in winter. When her father left her the beautiful house and all the contents of 1 Seymour Place, my mother installed Roberts there as her butler.

My first memories of Highclere are of the nurseries. On the second floor, tucked away at the far end of the corridor, life seemed safe and secure. Here I lived with my small sister Evelyn. We had a nanny to look after us and she was assisted by a nursery maid who washed and ironed our clothes. There was another maid whose job was to look after the fire, to clean the day and night nurseries and to wait on Nanny. Then we had another servant called the nursery footman who was responsible for bringing the meals upstairs.

We had plenty of plain food in the nursery and I well remember tapioca pudding and how I loathed it. For breakfast we usually had cereal of some sort or another which I also hated, and then bacon and eggs or fish, followed by toast and honey with milk to drink. We had nothing more, and who could have wanted it, until lunchtime.

After breakfast we were made tidy and sent down the backstairs to play outside. We were not allowed to use the front stairs as my father and mother always went on the principle that children should not be heard. They seldom came to visit us so we carried on with our nursery life quite undisturbed.

The morning activities might include a ride. When I was around the tender age of five, I was popped on to a small black Shetland pony and led round the garden by a very portly groom who panted and grunted to an extent which made me feel that at any moment he was going to blow up. This was not surprising as he was dressed in a pepper-and-salt riding coat with breeches to match, gaiters, a white starched stock around his neck and a black billycock hat perched on his head.

Some mornings I might ask Nanny if I could go and say hello to my friends in the kitchen. She always came up with the same answer: it entirely depended on whether they had time, whether they were busy or not. In those days in the kitchen there was a head chef, an under chef, two or three kitchenmaids and a scullery maid who did nothing but wash dishes. At one time, my father even had a curry cook imported from Ceylon. He stayed for the summer and when it began to get cold, he threw his hand in.

In the still-room, where all the breakfast trays for the guests were prepared, there was a very able Scottish maid who made scones and another maid whose sole responsibility was to make cakes. She would concoct the most delicious chocolate confections and huge sponges which were sometimes filled with apricot jam and covered with Marquis chocolate. These were greatly enjoyed by us – when we were lucky enough to get any – we usually got the crumbs which fell from the dining-room table, so to speak. If the servants were not too busy, they always seemed very pleased to see us and were extremely friendly and talkative. When we had looked at everything that was going on and had had a good poke round, as children do, we would be returned to our nursery quarters where Nanny would insist that we had a rest before lunch.

We had our lunch in the nursery with Nanny but if my parents had guests staying at Highclere, I would occasionally be sent for afterwards. I was dressed up for the occasion in my stiffest clothes and duly made my way to the dining-room feeling absolutely petrified. I would be told to shake hands with some of the guests, one of whom might offer me a chocolate. My mother, however, usually said, 'Don't give him that, for Heaven's sake, he'll be sick.' So I never got the chocolate, although I wanted it.

After a few minutes my mother would then say, 'You'll be wanting to go off for a nice long walk now. It will do you good and then you can get on with your lessons.' Thus I would be dismissed and hurried out of the room to find Nanny.

I was never allowed to keep a pet for the theory was that cats and dogs made messes and were, therefore, undesirable. I often longed for someone to play with for Eve was several years younger but it was never suggested that anyone of my age should come to stay. Occasionally we were allowed to have a party and some of the children who lived nearby would be brought by their nannies. But there never seemed anything very much to do, there were no organized games and the only part I really enjoyed was playing with balloons which we got out of crackers. How different it all was to the way in which my children and grandchildren have been brought up. There was little of the modern concept of affection between parent and child. We lived our sensible, dreary and orderly lives upstairs, whilst our parents carried on in their gregarious fashion below.

My parents enjoyed entertaining and there were always about a dozen people invited for Christmas. I remember being allowed to come down for dessert on Christmas Day. My sister and I walked round the table a couple of times and usually each guest gave us either a golden sovereign or a five shilling piece. On one occasion, a dear old boy called Seymour Fortescue handed me a crisp, new, five pound note. I was so surprised that I did not know what to do with it but I needn't have worried for it was promptly grabbed by my mother, who said, 'How kind, you must thank him profusely. I will put it in your money-box.' Of course, I never saw it again. Quite typical of the way in which children were treated in those days.

In the summer, we were taken to the seaside for six weeks. It was looked on as a hygienic exercise and we were usually packed off either to Cromer or Hunstanton, in Norfolk. At least we met other children there and amused ourselves by making sandcastles. Nanny, however, did not think some of the children were suitable playmates for me as she did not know their backgrounds. As far as I was concerned, if any of them helped me build good sandcastles, I did not care twopence if their fathers were dukes or dustmen!

Nanny took us one day to see the local lifeboat being launched and it was pulled into the sea by six huge horses. This was quite a thrill.

I had a governess who taught me to read and write and then graduated to having a tutor. When I was eight, I was sent off to my 'prep' school called Ludgrove. My tutor was detailed to take me to London and put me on the school train. On arrival at school we were met by Matron who checked up on the state of our bowels and our smallpox vaccination. She was very particular about all her charges cleaning their teeth twice a day but, curiously, we only had hot baths twice a week. I well remember comparing the very small towels we were given to the huge soft bath towels at Highclere. There were no Highclere breakfasts either! We always started off with something deadly dull such as porridge, without milk or cream and very little sugar. We were then given a sausage or, on other days, a little bacon. The theory was that it was a great mistake to give children a heavy meal before their lessons. We worked from 9 am to 1 pm with a short break at eleven o'clock for a glass of milk and one dry biscuit. To this day I have always thought it would have been no more expensive to give us each a couple of ginger nuts, which I have always enjoyed, rather than a cracker which jolly nearly broke a tooth each time we tried to masticate.

In 1911, I went to Impey's house at Eton, where I made many friends, one of the greatest of whom was Harry Kerr, Lord Greville's eldest son. Sadly, he, like so many of my contemporaries, was killed on the Somme.

On my arrival at Eton, I was shown to my room by our Dame, Miss Moss, a grey-haired woman always known to us as 'Pussy' Moss. She told me my neighbour would be Lord Blandford who subsequently became my great friend Bert Marlborough.

I was happy at Eton where I enjoyed playing fives, squash and boxing as a fly-weight. I got as far as being twelfth man in a cricket team known as Lower Sixpenny. From October to April I was also a regular follower of the Eton beagles.

I have frequently been asked when I first became interested in politics. Well, it was when I was at Eton aged about thirteen. Harry Kerr and I walked into Windsor one cold November afternoon and underneath the castle walls we heard a prospective Tory candidate addressing a crowd of about two hundred people.

'Finally, ladies and gentlemen,' he said, 'I have told you of all my aims and my hopes. One last word. I trust you will all vote for me – my father was a baron and my grandfather was a baron. . . .'

'What a ruddy shame your mother wasn't barren too!' a voice from the crowd shouted.

I had a fag master whose tea I fetched daily from Rowlands, the tuckshop in the town. When I returned to the house, I had to make three or four pieces of hot toast for him. I had an account at Rowlands but my father was unbelievably mean and only allowed me a credit of ninepence a day. I longed to have sausages and eggs and bacon as the other boys were doing, but they were far too expensive for my modest budget. I occasionally spent a week's money at one go and had a feast, then lived frugally for the rest of the week on what my housemaster provided. Sometimes my fag master asked me what I had for tea and when I told him cold curlew – all I could afford if I had already spent my allowance – he would take pity on me and tell me to buy some sausages and eggs and put it down to his account. This only happened very occasionally, if he was in a good mood, but I was very happy to eat the crumbs which fell from the rich man's table. During one holiday I tried telling my father that ninepence was not enough but this met with a very bad reception from him!

There were only a few boys who were allowed to have fags and some of these were members of Pop, an Eton society, and they wore braid round their coats and usually sported butterfly collars. They were very important people in their own right and were generally good at games such as cricket or fives, or they were master of the beagles or keeper of the Wall Game; in fact anything that they did better than the general run of boys at Eton or the tugs, which was the term applied to all those who were scholars and not the ordinary boys who went to housemasters. Members of Pop were allowed to cane inmates of their houses and used special canes with knots every six inches apart which were called Pop canes.

Although I quite enjoyed school, I missed the privacy and the wide open spaces of Highclere. It was such a joy to return in the holidays and be able to wander at will all over the estate.

One day, when I was in my teens, I went hunting with the Craven Hounds who were trying to find a fox near Milford Lake House. The coverts were full of rhododendron bushes in those days and it was pleasant to ride around those woods. On this particular occasion, a small pole about three feet high had been placed across one of the rides. I hopped over it on my pony and expected the huntsman to follow. He advanced at a slow trot towards it and the horse refused. He tried again and met with another refusal. I popped back over the pole, got behind him and gave the horse a damn good crack with my whip, shouting, 'Go on, George!'

This time the horse leapt forward and the poor man landed on its neck and nearly fell off.

'You didn't ought to have done that, m'lord,' he said, 'I might have 'ad a nasty fall.'

We went to the seaside for our health with Nanny when we were small but we were not taken when we were older. I spent all my school holidays at Highclere with my sister for in those days children were seldom taken abroad by their parents. The idea of an annual fortnight's jaunt to some foreign beach was unheard of. My father travelled abroad a great deal, not only in the East but all over Europe, especially in the Balkans. My mother frequently visited France and Italy but she did not take us with her.

I would usually find a tutor in residence on my return from school who would make me study daily. Lessons done, I escaped into the garden as soon as I could. We never had any friends of our own age to stay for it never occurred to us that we would be allowed to have them, so we never asked any. I can't recollect ever going to another boy's home to stay with him. I never went to lunch or tea with anyone of my own age after Nanny left.

Still there was always riding, hunting or shooting with which to amuse myself. Even if I was not allowed to participate, I could always watch. During school holidays I often stood by my father when he held shooting parties. On one occasion, General Sir Redvers Buller, the hero of Ladysmith during the Boer War, peppered one of the beaters when shooting at a low pheasant.

The beater complained to my father that he had been

shot by one of his guests and pointed his finger at the general.

'What is that man saying about me?' demanded the general.

'Actually,' said Papa somewhat nervously, 'he says that you tickled him up when you were shooting that hen.'

Bristling with rage, the general roared, 'Good God! What the devil is he making a fuss about? They are only pellets, not shrapnel!'

After leaving Eton, I went to a 'crammer' for about six months to prepare for the entrance exam into Sandhurst. Eventually I passed into the Royal Military College – the fact that my father was a great friend of Lord Kitchener was, I'm ashamed to say, of immense help!

I spent six months at Sandhurst during which time I worked hard and played hard. I was then commissioned into the 7th Queen's Own Hussars and posted to Newbridge in Ireland.

On arrival, I was interviewed by a somewhat elderly long-retired member of the regiment.

'Delighted to welcome you here, my boy', he said. 'Now, a question I always ask young officers ... how many times have you had clap?'

'Never,' I assured him hastily.

'Good Lord! Are you serious? You're quite normal, I suppose?'

'Indeed I am!' I replied.

2

King Tut's Treasures

IN 1923 I SPENT Christmas at Blenheim Palace with the Marlboroughs and amongst the guests was Winston Churchill, a good friend of mine, and he asked me to tell him about my father. Winston was Chancellor of the Exchequer at that time and I happened to end the story by saying that my father died on 5 April 1923. Winston gave a little chuckle and commented, 'How very civil of him.'

For the benefit of anybody who does not quite understand what a clever remark that was, I must point out that in England the financial year ends on 5 April, and as such, many of the complicated affairs like death duties were much simplified. In those days the British government gave everyone nine months' grace in which to pay whatever they owed and if these charges had not been met, the laggards were forced to pay one per cent over the Bank Rate until the whole of the dues had been handed over.

But what had particularly interested Winston had been the story of my father's discovery of King Tutankhamun's tomb. It had all begun because of my father's health problems.

My father had a somewhat weak chest and was told

by his medical advisers that he must winter every year in a warm climate. He decided in 1902 to go to Egypt about the middle of January when the pheasant shooting had ended.

When he arrived in Cairo, Lord Cromer, who was our Resident at the time, told him that if he was going out to Egypt regularly, he would be bored to tears having nothing to do. He thought my father should have a hobby and suggested archaeology. He told him about a young man, Howard Carter, who had had a disagreement with his boss and, as a result, had to leave the Egyptian Civil Service. Cromer knew that Carter believed that somewhere in the Valley of the Kings the remaining tomb of the pharaohs was yet to be found.

Cromer arranged for Carter to meet my father at the residency the following morning at 10 am. After introducing them, he left them alone to discuss such matters as the salary that Carter would receive. When working as a government official he had received the princely sum of £300 per annum! My dear father proposed to pay him a salary of £100 a quarter which upped his wages by £100 per year.

Papa and Howard, having established the best of relationships, decided that they would start digging systematically until they found the tomb. In those days, they employed approximately four hundred fellaheens who were paid a very small sum of money, not much more than five piastres per day.

Carter bought Egyptian antiques, scarabs and other valuable pieces in the bazaar and also through private dealers and resold them for considerable profit. These activities helped the budget for the excavations.

Carter worked like a beaver all through the year and my father usually went out with my mother each February for a stay of about a couple of months. They booked in at the Winter Palace in Luxor, riding out on donkeys to Carter's house at El Gurnah which was his pad in the Valley of the Kings.

The excavations went on merry as a marriage bell until shortly after the outbreak of hostilities in 1914. My father was told that it would be impossible to go on digging because at that time the Duke of Westminster, with his armoured cars, was fighting the Senussi and so all work in that area had to cease until the war ended.

Whilst Howard Carter and my father restlessly waited for hostilities to cease, Papa became keenly interested in the occult. When I returned from Mesopotamia, I spent most of my month's leave at Highclere with my family and Howard Carter. I well remember proceeding to the East Anglia bedroom with my sister Eve, my father, Howard Carter, Helen Cunliffe-Owen and Louis Steele, who was a brilliant photographer domiciled in Portsmouth, for a séance.

Steele delivered a sort of incantation to Lady Cunliffe-Owen who soon went into a trance and spoke in Coptic, a language which only Howard Carter understood. After a few minutes, she opened her eyes and resumed the conversation in which she had been engaged before going into a trance.

Eve was then put into a trance but she was so overcome by the experience that she had to go into a nursing home in London for a fortnight's rest.

To round off that session, my father said, 'If we sit

round the table holding hands, I believe we shall achieve a levitation.'

'What does he mean?' I whispered to my sister.

'I think he hopes the flowers on the table will rise several feet into the air,' she replied and they did.

The war over, excavations could now begin again. But by that time expenses had risen and my father told Carter that things were quite different from when they started. Carter, in reply, explained that so much of the donkey work had been done that he was confident of hitting the jackpot in another year or two. My father agreed that digging should continue but emphasized that there must be a time limit of not more than about three years.

As time went on, Papa became more and more grumpy and said to Carter, 'It is now 1921 and my patience and money are rapidly running out! I give you one more year and that is my last word.'

'Well,' replied Carter, 'all I can say is that I'll do my damnedest to dig him up.'

On 10 November 1922, Carter's foreman rushed up, greatly excited, to say that he had found steps leading up to what he felt sure was the tomb. Carter was thrilled when he saw the sight he had longed to see. He sent a cable to my father asking him to come out as soon as possible.

Papa, who was busily engaged with his shooting parties, sent him a telegram to say that he would arrive with my sister around 22 November. They went for a brief visit and he satisfied himself that the tomb had not been pillaged. Carter begged him to come back in February when everything would be ready for the opening of the tomb.

The opening ceremony took place in February 1923, in front of the world's press and many distinguished visitors including the King of the Belgians and several members of the Egyptian government. This historic occasion was much heralded throughout the world and gave enormous pleasure both to the spectators on the spot and to the millions of readers of the international press.

Shortly afterwards my poor old parent was bitten by a mosquito when sleeping. The following morning, as he always shaved with a cut-throat razor, he cut the top of the mosquito bite but considered it unnecessary to do anything other than place a bit of cottonwool dabbed in iodine onto the wound. He and Eve left as usual for the tomb and when they got there, entered and took part in all the activities that were going on under Carter's direction. As was their custom, they lunched at El Gurnah, Carter's home, and after the meal, my father said he felt very shivery and came to the conclusion that he had a temperature. My sister took him back to the Winter Palace Hotel in Luxor, gave him the usual aspirin and hot toddy and hoped that in the morning he would have completely recovered.

Next morning, he emerged, saying that his temperature was sub-normal and they returned to the tomb. By midday he told my sister that he felt ghastly, but this time, with her usual prescience, she had taken a thermometer with her. She found he had a raging temperature, to wit, 102 degrees and immediately took him back to Luxor and arranged that they should catch the midnight train to Cairo and warned the manager of the Continental Hotel that he was responsible for collecting the best talent available in the medical profession to meet them as soon as they arrived.

All this duly took place and a cable was sent to my mother and Dr Johnson, his personal physician who was in London, to proceed to his bedside as quickly as possible as he was suffering from blood-poisoning. My mother gallantly chartered a Pussmoth and accompanied by 'Johnny', flying via Marseilles, Brindisi, etc., reached Cairo in record time. My father meanwhile had slowly recovered and after about ten days he was allowed to sit up in his room. Unfortunately, this one occasion brought on pneumonia and he returned to bed gravely ill. He passed away at five minutes to two in the morning of 5 April 1923. My father's bitch, Susie sat up on her hind legs, howled like a wolf at five minutes to four on the night that he died and fell back dead in her basket at Highclere and at a later date, Howard Carter's canary was swallowed by a cobra. These occurrences gave rise to the birth of the legend of the Curse of King Tutankhamun.

I have often been asked if I believe in the Curse and my reply is invariably the same, I have said and repeat, 'I neither believe nor do I disbelieve in these strange happenings for which no logical explanation has ever been offered and in my judgement, this will be the case for ever. Carter lived to a ripe old age, he frequently visited me and as far as I know, died of cirrhosis of the liver, which is not uncommon for a man who had spent

most of his life in the Middle East. My mother lived to
be ninety-two and might well be alive today had she
not had the misfortune to choke on a piece of gristle
when eating chicken for her lunch. I am in my eighty-
first year and still *compos mentis.*'

In the autumn of 1976, I was invited to go to Washington by the Exxon Corporation to take part in the
opening ceremony of the Egyptian Collection which
they had brought over at great expense for a two-year
tour of the United States.

This exhibition contained some of the choicest of
my father's discoveries for which, I regret to say, he
was never given any credit. The world must never
forget that it was my father's money and Howard
Carter's faith and determination which resulted in
the discovery of the tomb in the autumn of 1922 with
most of its treasures intact. The discovery has brought
enormous revenue throughout the years to the
Egyptian government.

My friend, Paul Mellon, was surprised and somewhat shocked that I was not seated at the top table at
the dinner which was given on the night before the
official opening. The seating arrangements had
nothing whatever to do with Paul. It was a sad moment
for me to hear Henry Kissinger making a long speech,
chiefly of a political nature, and even more galling
when the Egyptian ambassador replied at great length
and never once did he make any reference to my father
or Howard Carter who had been the architect of this
marvellous discovery.

When talking that evening to the Egyptian ambassador, I told him I thought the Egyptian government of
that time had behaved very badly. He replied that,
of course, he himself had hardly seen the light of
day when this event occurred. He went on to say,
'The people of that era were quite different to our
present administration now that we have become a
republic.'

Immediately after my father's death on 5 April 1923,
the Egyptian government had decreed that all treasures
found in the tomb of King Tut were the property of the
Egyptian government. They even placed barbed wire
round the tomb which was guarded by soldiers under
the command of an Englishman, seconded to the military police, by name Corporal Adamson. Howard
Carter was denied access for six weeks. The government also stated that the licence to dig had been issued
annually to my father and that his heirs and successors
were not entitled to any of the treasures found in the
tomb, thus ensuring that the entire contents were the
property of the Egyptian government.

I immediately consulted Sir Edward Marshall Hall
KC, as to whether or not this action of theirs was legal,
because, had my father lived, he would have been
entitled to a duplicate of every article found in the
tomb. Marshall Hall explained to me that if I were to
contest this edict in the mixed courts in Cairo, I would
have no chance of success. Of the five judges who
would hear the case, an Englishman, a Frenchman,
an Italian and two Egyptians, the Egyptians would

be instructed as to the verdict they should return and to make quite certain of the outcome, the Italian would be bought! The odds, therefore, would be six to four against me before the case was even heard.

Acting on his advice, I decided it was best to forget this distasteful affair.

I paid Carter a salary of £5,000 a year for the next seven years and he packed all the relics with the greatest possible care and eventually uncrated them in Cairo, handing them over in mint condition to the curator of the Cairo Museum. Before the discovery of the tomb, entry to the Cairo Museum cost five piastres and the building was nearly always empty. From the moment that the objects found in the tomb were displayed to the public gaze, the museum was thronged by visitors who were happy to pay twenty-five piastres for the privilege of seeing these wonderful things.

You can imagine my feelings, kind reader, when seven years later in 1930 I went to Cairo and was asked to visit King Farouk at the Abdin Palace. Whilst there, I was offered – and promptly declined – The Grand Cordon of the Order of the Nile. This decoration was known to all the soldiers of that era as 'The Nile Boil'.

I protested vehemently to the King about the way his government had treated me. I stressed that, in all fairness, they should refund me the £35,000 which I had paid on their behalf to Howard Carter for his invaluable services. I ended my interview by urging the King to telephone his Minister of Finance to send a cheque to the Semiramis Hotel as I was leaving for England the following morning.

His Majesty picked up the telephone and did as I asked. The cheque was delivered to my hotel that evening and I was delighted to see the return of my outlay, although not a single piastre was added by way of interest to this long-standing debt.

Many years later at the height of the Suez controversy in the 1950s, I received a letter from the curator of the Cairo Museum asking me if I would open the new wing which had just been added to the museum for the purpose of housing the Tutankhamun treasure. Not wishing to cause any political controversy between the United Kingdom and Egypt, I telephoned Anthony Eden, who was the Prime Minister at the time, to ask his opinion as he was a good pal of mine.

I explained the situation to him and said that I was most anxious not to embarrass him or his government.

'My dear Porchey,' he said, 'of course you have a perfect right to go if you wish. It would obviously be rather an embarrassment to us, but please don't let that stop you.'

I need hardly say that I promptly declined.

The idea of the Curse of Tutankhamun still fascinates people and it certainly seemed to intrigue Americans when the treasures were on view in the United States. I was asked many more questions about the curse on television and on radio than I was asked about the antiques themselves and great interest was shown in what had happened to the archaeologists since the uncovering of the tomb.

When I was in Washington two days after the official opening, I had just finished a long television interview with John Lyndsay, ex-Mayor of New York, and was leaving for lunch when I overheard a young American girl, aged about eighteen, say to her mother as they looked at a glass case containing a small gold head of Queen Nefertiti, 'Mummy, if I had a rich lover, I'd get him to buy me that and I could wear it in the lapel of my coat or in a turban, couldn't I?'

Whereupon 'Mummy' replied, somewhat scathingly, to her spotty teenaged daughter, 'Honey, if I had a rich lover, I'd do something very different. I'd get hold of the son of the guy who found King Tut – I believe he's here now – and I'd ask him to tell me the full story of the Curse. That would interest me more than anything else I can think of concerning all these wonderful objects we have looked at this morning.'

More recently, controversy has switched to the original opening ceremony at the tomb in 1923. A new book has been published on this subject by Thomas Hoving entitled *The Untold Story*. When this book appeared in England, Southern Television made a programme on the subject for they had managed to trace Corporal Adamson, the commander of the guard placed round the newly-discovered tomb. The television interviewer asked Corporal Adamson his opinion of the various allegations made in the book. By chance I happened to be watching and, needless to say, I was delighted to hear Corporal Adamson explain that he had slept every night for six weeks over the hole by which anyone must get in or out of the tomb, therefore it would have been impossible for my father or Howard Carter to have taken anything out at night during this time without his knowledge.

3
A Warning to Unwary Males

WHEN MY FRIEND Tommy Frost, who had retired from the 15th Hussars, suggested that, should I get leave and join him in London, he would take me out on the town, I readily agreed. I gave him a date when I would be free and he collected me from my parents' house, accompanied by his very attractive girlfriend. A beautiful girl was brought along as my partner. She informed me that her husband was a naval officer who at that time was serving on a gunboat on the Yangtze River in China. She proved to be a lovely dancer and seemed a delectable dish.

After we left the Savoy, Tommy went off with his girl and my girl asked me to have a nightcap at her flat in Piccadilly. On arrival there, I found a nice cold supper laid out on a small table, with a magnum of champagne on ice. As we had had an excellent dinner, neither of us felt hungry. All I was interested in was how quickly I could get this dreamboat into bed. She was just as willing and in a short time we were in her double bed.

About an hour later, I was awakened by a dig in the ribs. My beautiful companion was holding a small bottle in her hand and announced that her husband was in the next room and that he was a professional boxer. She told me to hand over everything I had, such as cash, cuff-links and cigarette case and threatened that she would throw vitriol in my face if I did not comply immediately with her instructions.

By this time I was shaking like a jelly and with trembling fingers I dressed as quickly as I could. I then handed over the jewellery, such as it was, managing to secrete a twenty pound note in my waistcoat pocket. She seemed thoroughly angry that I had so little money and told me to clear out and keep my mouth shut.

While walking home to No. 1 Seymour Place, I met a kindly policeman and told him what had happened to me. He replied that the police had had many complaints about the old badger game in Piccadilly but as far as he knew, none of the victims had ever had the guts to bring a case to court. He strongly advised me to look on the incident as a sad experience and to take no further action. I took his wise advice and warned Tommy Frost to be careful of his girlfriend's companions.

I had a charming friend who lived in Kenya and as I had a moment to spare from a visit to the War Office, I dropped into the Ritz Hotel and wrote a letter to her and suddenly I remembered that I didn't know her address. I promptly sent a reply-paid cable to a mutual friend, who was also an admirer of hers, Donald Haldeman, asking him if he knew Phyllis's address. The following day I received a reply – the shortest I have ever received – namely one word, 'YES'.

By a curious coincidence, on the very same day, I happened to run into her ex-husband on my way to White's. He was rightly nicknamed 'The Borstal Boy'. They had continually quarrelled, chiefly on the score of marital infidelities and after one of these dramas, when sitting in the carriage of a train at the Gare du Nord, Phyllis had shot him with a small calibre pistol, but only winged him.

When I showed him Donald's cable, he said he knew where she lived and would tell me for a fiver. Needless to say, I did not part with any money and got her address from another source.

Phyllis died in Kenya in 1942 and I received the last letter she ever wrote to anybody, which was a poignant reminder of a delightful friendship.

A middle-aged American lady with three married children asked if I would agree to become her next husband. I told her that I would not make a very good husband; nevertheless she replied that she would be prepared to risk it, telling me at the same time that she was worth at least five hundred million sterling and pulled out a list of her investments which made my head reel.

A thought then struck her. 'Listen honey,' she said, 'if we were to get married, would I become an earless?'

I told her that she would become a countess, to which she replied, 'I don't think much of that – counts are two a penny over here.'

I finally convinced her that I was not for sale and she

said that she would like to buy me a little present. We
went to Cartier in New York, where she asked to see
a tray of evening watches. They were all platinum,
encrusted with diamonds, emeralds or rubies, costing
in the region of $6,000 each. She asked me to choose
one but I told her I would not be seen dead in a ditch
with a watch of that type as they were only suitable for
gigolos!

Disappointed that I refused her offer of a watch, she
asked if there was anything she could do for me. As I
had very little foreign currency – this was just after the
Second World War – I told her I'd be grateful if she
could give me $300 to settle my hotel bill. She immedi-
ately pulled out three $100 bills from her handbag
which was stuffed with notes to the tune of about
fifteen thousand bucks.

Finally, she enquired if I knew of any other bachelor
earl, with a castle, who might like to marry her. I
contacted my good friend, Alan Inverclyde, an
impoverished peer, and he agreed to invite her to stay
at his castle near Edinburgh.

I then forgot all about her until one day she called me
up at the Ritz.

'I didn't think much of your friend's castle. It would
cost me around six million dollars to make it habitable
and, believe it or not, that guy never even made a
pass at me! I would also remind you that you owe me
three hundred bucks which you *borrowed* in New
York.'

I took a deep breath, counted five, and told her I
would send the money to Claridge's immediately.

By a strange coincidence, the next time I saw her was
when staying with Charlie Munn at Amado in Palm

Beach, Florida. On the day of my arrival, Charlie told me that we were dining with Mr and Mrs X who were giving a large party in my honour. To my horror, I found that my hostess was my old friend who had remarried and her new name had conveyed nothing to me.

She died about six months later, followed shortly by her husband. Some people said at the time that it was a photo-finish to the grave!

4
Early Days

RETURNING FROM THE campaign in Mesopotamia at the end of the First World War, a small cadre of the regiment had a dreary journey from Basra to Suez, via Bombay. I then had to do everything I could to expedite our passage through the canal so that we could meet up with another ship at Port Said which, we hoped, would take us back to England as quickly as possible.

When I got off the ship at Suez, I was pestered by one of those cursed pimps who always wanted to sell you filthy pictures or some other form of pornography. On this particular occasion, I was really irritated as I had to get on with the business in hand. So, when the beast stopped me and said, 'You like to have my sister?' I shouted, 'Certainly not! All I want is the harbour master.'

'Harbour master', he repeated, 'he velly, velly expensive.'

On arrival in England I ran into Lord Settrington, a young man of great charm who was one of the best-looking human beings I have ever seen. He was a great friend and, had he survived a wound received in action, he would have succeeded to the title of Duke of Richmond and Gordon. During the war he had been in the Brigade of Guards and had been taken prisoner soon after the outbreak of hostilities. We decided to have dinner together at the Savoy and to talk over old times. At the end of our celebration, Charlie said, 'I feel very badly about having done nothing in the war.'

'What do you mean you have done nothing?' I replied. 'You had the misfortune to be taken prisoner and that was that!'

'In point of fact,' he said, 'I've seen no active service so I'm joining General Sadler Jackson as his ADC. He commands troops who are going to fight the Bolsheviks in support of General Wrangel who leads the White Russian forces in that area.'

'Do think again, Charlie,' I said. 'I hate the idea of you taking part in any further fighting.'

He refused to take my advice and, to my sorrow, I learned later that he had been shot and badly wounded by a sniper when on a reconnaissance in a forest. He was rushed to a field hospital where the bullet was removed but, alas, as so often happened in those days, gangrene set in and he passed away within a week.

I had an interesting experience whilst in Baghdad on an intelligence course for I met Dimitri, one of the two people who had disposed of Rasputin, the greasy long-haired monk who had such influence over the

Tsarina because he had persuaded her that he had
occult powers and could cure her son, the little
Tsarevitch, who suffered from haemophilia.

I found the Grand Duke Dimitri a most charming
and erudite man. We dined alone one evening and he
told me how Rasputin had become influential at court
and thereby incurred Dimitri's enmity and that of
Prince Yusupoff, both of whom were devoted to the
ruler and his family. They emanated from the best-
known families of the Russian aristocracy.

Dimitri and Yusupoff had talked over the fate of
Rasputin in great detail and had decided that the best
way to resolve this horrible situation was to do away
with him as quickly as possible by some means or
other.

In the end, it was decided that Prince Yusupoff
should shoot Rasputin in his house, put his body on a
sleigh and, at dead of night, he and Dimitri would take
the corpse and throw it into the Neva. The river was
frozen at that time and they had to break the ice with
pickaxes and push the body through the hole they had
made. Luckily, the aperture froze quickly and, as far as
the world was concerned, Rasputin had disappeared
without trace.

I stayed on in the 7th Hussars after the war was over
and so was with the regiment in Liverpool helping the
police keep order during the General Strike. We had
erected a sandbag barricade to close Union Street. The
troopers, who were mostly raw recruits, had been
issued with five rounds of ammunition in case events

became serious and out of control, but I told my troop sergeant that no rifles were to be loaded unless I gave a specific order to that effect.

On this cold, grey autumn day, I saw a large mob of men and women coming towards our position, mostly carrying flags with slogans, and when they got within about ten yards of the sandbags I thought it wise to jump on top of the parapet and say a few words which might mollify them. I put my hand up and everybody came to a halt. I shouted to them that I thought a horse of mine called Gracious Gift, ridden by Tommy Hulme, would win the Novices' Chase to be run at Manchester at 3 pm. This was loudly applauded and they dispersed without any further bother.

The sequel was even more amusing because my horse, which started at 11–8 against, duly won, and the following day a very orderly procession of delighted punters called on me asking to be told another winner.

I replied sadly that I did not know any more but the best winner for all would be for them to go back to work and we could then return to barracks.

Although I was stationed at York for some time, I managed to get frequent leave and would come to London whenever I could. Despite the General Strike and all its attendant problems, the 1920s were full of vitality. It was the fashion to hold large parties and balls in private houses such as Londonderry House, Norfolk House and even in my mother's lovely house at Seymour Place.

The scenario was much the same on every occasion.

There would be perhaps ten dances, then supper, and then another ten dances. Supper was generally a gargantuan meal with lovely fat Egyptian quails, lobster galore, various cold meats as well as mountains of hot salmon kedgeree. If anyone had any room left, they could finish off by having raspberries and cream or fresh peaches from the hothouse, according to the season. This would be washed down by fine champagne, excellent port and old brandy. Having had this splendid collation, there was no need for what is called 'breakfast' at today's parties which are a pale shadow of those that took place half a century ago.

The rules about dress were strictly adhered to in those days. If dining at a club, it was the custom to wear a dinner jacket. A tail coat and white tie were generally worn when going to the theatre, a restaurant, or any other activity one went to with friends. If invited to a ball, it was customary to wear white kid gloves when dancing as ladies, quite rightly, did not like having their dresses soiled by sweaty hands!

Afterwards some of us might wander along to a nightclub. I've never been very keen on them as I'm an early-to-bed man myself, but I would go anywhere to hear Louis Armstrong and his band. He was a great guy and always cheerful.

As soon as he saw me, he would shout, 'Come on, boys, the lord wants "Birth of the Blues", that's his signature.'

Turning to me, he would say, 'You got a super dame with you tonight. Any other requests you just tell us. With a dish like that, you got to have all we can give.'

On these occasions I would usually stay at one of my clubs for what was left of the night for I never possessed my own London house. There was a time when I could get a bedroom and an excellent breakfast at the Portland, which was then situated in Charles Street, for £1 a night. It really was remarkably good value even in those days. Nor were annual subscriptions exorbitant then so it was not unusual to belong to four or five clubs as I did.

My father was a member of the Turf. I remember his being very anxious that I should be elected as early as possible. He explained that if I was not elected by the age of twenty-one, it was probable that I would have done something to annoy some of the members and might well be blackballed. He therefore took infinite pains to make sure that I was elected before I came of age.

I also joined the Cavalry Club and one founded by dear old Herbert Buckmaster for cavalry officers, as a counterpart to the Guard's Club, which was called Buck's. Buckmaster was married to Gladys Cooper and was the father of the present Mrs Robert Morley. I belonged to Buck's for many years but I resigned from most of my clubs and am now left with only two, White's and the Portland.

I had a lot of fun at the Portland and learned to hold my own at the bridge table. After a good rubber one day, my old friend Francis Queensberry, the most generous of men, said to me: 'If you go on as you're going, old boy, the gals will get all your portable property. I wish to God you'd leave them alone and let us have a chance of getting some of your boodle which would then be in much better 'ands than if you'd given it to the gals.'

As I have said, I never owned a house in London so, if I did not stay at one of my clubs, I would return to Highclere. The train service was so good in the twenties that if I had to go to London for some reason during the day I could be up in under an hour. Whenever possible I preferred to sleep at home. I would get my chauffeur, Edward Trotman, who was very deaf, to take me to Newbury by car and would arrange for him to meet me on my return. One day I said to him at the top of my voice, 'I'll be back on the six o'clock train.'

To which he replied, 'I don't think it will, the glass is very 'igh.'

My mother, who was left a vast fortune by Alfred de Rothschild, travelled to Scotland by train and, in her usual extravagant manner, always gave £5 to the guard and the engine driver and £10 to the stationmaster who always saw her off and met her on her return as he, quite rightly, saw this as a golden opportunity which he must not miss! She was such a spendthrift that I had to rescue her from financial difficulties on two or three occasions. The last time, against my better judgement, I was persuaded that I should chip in another £70,000 to save her from being declared bankrupt. On the strength of this, my mother gave a party such as I have never seen. When I remonstrated with her, she replied, 'It's the very best way to stave off my creditors. A magnificent party like this will be written up in all the papers. I don't think I'll have any trouble for at least a year!'

Besides balls and parties, we would while away the evenings by playing cards, dining out or going to the theatre. I particularly enjoyed a good laugh which could often be found at a farce or a review. C. B. Cochran and Noel Coward were putting on good plays at that time and excellent fun could be gained from going to see them. But I never ceased to be surprised at the sort of jokes which managed to give pleasure to millions of people.

At one time, at the Alhambra, Harry Tate came on the stage with a tiny caddy carrying a huge bag of golf clubs. The caddy would place a tee on the stage with a golf ball on top of it and hand a driver to Tate who would look at the ball in a quizzical fashion.

The caddy then turned to him and said, 'Address the ball.'

Harry took off his little Glengarry and said, 'Good morning, ball.'

Would you believe it, that brought the house down! They cheered and clapped to the echo and this went on night after night. It was by far the most popular item in the whole show which ran for a very long time. As my father frequently said to me, 'Forty fools are born daily for one wise man to live upon.'

I have always loved the theatre which I suppose accounts for my interest in television now that I am in the sear and yellow. I have also always enjoyed playing bridge. I was playing one night with Charlie Londonderry, Cardy Montagu and Joe Whitburn when a footman came into the room right in the middle of the rubber and said, 'Your lordship is wanted on the telephone.'

When I asked who it was, he told me it was the editor of the *Yorkshire Post* who said it was most important that he should speak to me.

'I can't be bothered just now, tell him to call back later.'

'Don't do that,' said my friends, 'go and see what he wants.'

I went to the telephone and when the gentleman on the other end said, 'Am I speaking to Lord Carnarvon?'

I replied, 'You certainly are, who are you?'

'I am the editor of the *Yorkshire Post*,' he said, 'and I particularly wish to speak to you because we have inadvertently printed a story this morning which stated that your lordship had just been discharged from bankruptcy. We realized later that we had made a mistake when we made enquiries from the Press Association.'

Apparently a clerk in their office had written Carnarvon when he meant to write Carnwarth, as the Earl of Carnwarth had indeed been discharged from bankruptcy.

The editor continued, 'We are publishing a complete apology on the front page tomorrow explaining everything. Mr Rupert Becket, who owns this paper, asks you to please accept his personal apologies for any inconvenience this may have caused you.'

I thought pretty quickly and said, 'Please tell Mr

Becket that I accept his apologies and it is very kind of him to have sent this message but I can do nothing about the matter as it is already in the hands of my solicitors!'

I returned to my game of cards and when we had finished playing I told my friends what had happened.

My dear friend Cardy said to me, 'I can tell you the ideal firm of solicitors to handle this matter for you. I suggest you call them up early tomorrow morning, make an appointment to see them and explain the whole thing.'

The firm, to my joy, were called Cohen, Swizzler and Cohen. (Perhaps at this point I should remind the reader that I have Jewish blood in my veins.) I did as Cardy suggested and went up to see Mr Cohen, Mr Swizzler having joined the great majority. They had a seedy little office in the Strand and I had hardly got into the room before Mr Cohen, a typical little redhaired Jew aged about sixty, said, 'My lord, my lord, I've already got hold of several papers and they've all carried the story. We're in for a lovely time. I've still to get through to Ireland and I'm sure I shall find a lot more there. We got the *Scotsman* too, quite a harvest!'

I listened spellbound while another little redhaired Jew brought each of us a cup of coffee.

Then came the great moment...

'My lord, I've thought of something,' said Mr Cohen, 'you don't want to be bothered with any of this. I'll do it all for you. I've the following suggestion to make. I'll give you a cheque for say, £12,000, and I'll take whatever else I may get for my services.'

'Fair enough,' I said, 'but tell me, Mr Cohen, what do you expect to get for your services?'

'My lord,' he said, 'some of these are little tiddlers I'll do well if I get £300 out of them. Some of the bigger fish I might get £3,000 – that's the beauty of it, you don't know. It's a kind of gamble. If I make £3,000 net for myself, I'll be very satisfied.'

I told him that I fully expected he would do even better than he suggested. I pocketed his cheque for £12,000 and went away whistling 'Pennies from Heaven'.

5
Stewardship Succession

IN THE LAST thirty years, this castle has been burgled no less than three times. I have lost a great deal of silver and there is now very little left to interest any would-be thief but, mercifully, so far the pictures are intact.

In my dining-room there is a picture of Charles I on a white horse by Van Dyck. There are two identical pictures, one in Windsor Castle and one at Warwick Castle. Van Dyck had a great many pupils and I am told that for a canvas that size, he would have had four pupils working on it. He had a large barn-like structure in Warwickshire and he and his adjutant, a very fine painter affectionately known as 'Old Stone', were in the habit of going round daily, helping and commenting to the pupils on the many canvases on which they were working. For instance, the maestro would perhaps take a brush from one of them and touch up the knee of the white horse and point out that there was not the right highlight on it. This was a long and tedious process but, in the end, he did turn out a great many paintings. How many will never be known as many of these works of art, signed by Van Dyck, were in fact painted by 'Old Stone'.

My picture of Charles I came from an old manor

house in Wiltshire which has since been pulled down but which once formed part of the Carnarvon estates. At some time the painting had been taken out of its frame and rolled up. It was then forgotten and ended up as a prop for a long ladder leading to a hayloft. One day a farmhand dislodged the ladder and knocked over the support. He unrolled the canvas and saw that it had some sort of picture on it so he informed our agent. There were two great holes in it but luckily these were in a dark background section. Eventually it was sent to London to be carefully repaired, cleaned and restored to its pristine glory and it has hung ever since in the present position in my dining-room.

There is a miniature hanging in the same room, indubitably painted by Van Dyck himself, of the huge canvas which covers the Cube Room at Wilton. In it are the various people who form the nucleus of the picture at Wilton. Van Dyck gave a similar miniature to all the members of the house of Herbert who figured in the canvas at Wilton. The three cherubs in the clouds are meant to represent children who died at birth. This picture was donated to my ancestor in 1801 and herewith is a reproduction of the letter he received:

My Lord, You will be surprised at receiving a letter from one who has the honour of being related to your Lordship, although unknown to you. I should not have troubled you had I not in my possession a very valuable miniature the same as the family picture at Wilton, painted by Van Dyck himself and given by Philip, Earl of Pembroke, to his son when he married the daughter of Sir Henry Speller, whose son married the Duke of Leed's daughter. My father was a son of theirs and I, being the last of the family, am unwilling that the picture should leave the Herberts. I request your Lordship's acceptance of it. Your Lordship's obedient servant, Anne Herbert.

Another picture of interest is a three-quarter-length portrait of Anne Clifford, Countess of Dorset, Pembroke and Montgomery. She is seated in a chair wearing a black dress with a pearl necklace and the picture is painted by Van Dyck. This lovely lady was married successively to Richard, 2nd Earl of Dorset, and then to Philip, 4th Earl of Pembroke.

In a letter she wrote as follows: 'These two lords of mine to whom I was by divine providence married were, in their several kinds, as worthy noblemen as any there were in the Kingdom, yet it was my misfortune to have contradictions and crosses with both of them.'

The good lady found that her first husband, poor man, was sterile. After a while, she met the Earl of Lonsdale who carried her off to his home in Westmorland and she was installed at Lowther Castle as his mistress. About two and a half years later, he sent her back to her husband accompanied by her son with the following letter addressed to Lord Dorset:

My Lord, Today by stage-coach I return to your Lordship her Ladyship with her bastard son who is a bonny boy. I feel sure that as you are unable to beget a son from your loins, you will accept this child to become your heir and, if you agree, I am confident he will do justice to your Lordship's title.

The Earl of Dorset certainly acted very honourably. He replied to Lonsdale that his wife had returned to him in splendid spirits and that he liked her boy very much and had made him his legal heir. This was a great feather in Anne's cap. She had proved herself to be a good mother and, as a result of her liaison with Lonsdale, she succeeded in keeping the Earldom of Dorset from extinction.

In the smoking-room at Highclere, there hangs a picture, painted by Sir William Beechy, of the family of the 1st Earl of Carnarvon. The three sons, the Hon. Charles, William and George Herbert, are shown with their dog Pincher and are beautifully painted, two of the boys wearing red suits and the third a green one. Their sister, Lady Frances Herbert, who was at finishing school in Florence when the picture was painted, made a tremendous fuss on her return because she was not included in the family portrait. Beechy offered to paint her full length in any costume she chose to wear for the sum of thirty guineas rather than ruin the composition of a well-balanced portrait. Her father, however, weakly gave in to her tantrums and insisted that she should be allowed to take her place in the group as she was his eldest child.

My father was so annoyed about this that he asked Joe Duveen in 1918 if this girl could be removed from the painting in any way. Duveen replied that it was quite impossible to do so because the pigments that were in use at that period were totally different to those used today.

I have asked many of my guests over the last sixty years whether they could see anything wrong with the composition of this picture. Very few have recognized the problem. Amongst those who did so was Harry Hambleden, my cousin, and Oswald Birley, the well-known artist.

My favourite picture in the smoking-room is 'The Laughing Philosopher' by Annibale Carracci, an extremely clever artist who painted most of his masterpieces in Italy. The man in the painting that I have is so true to life and looks so happy that when I feel depressed, I cheer up instantly by gazing on his smiling face!

Amongst my furniture I have one or two items which are of considerable interest. There is a chair and table in the library on which Napoleon signed his abdication when he was a prisoner on the Island of Elba. On each arm of the chair there are many scratches which were said to have been made by the emperor when he was dictating letters to his secretary. My readers must remember that in 1800 shorthand did not exist and everything had to be taken down in ink with the aid of a quill pen. If the long-suffering secretary asked his master to stop as he had been dictating too quickly for everything to be written down, Napoleon displayed his irritability by making the scratches with his nails. I think there might well be some truth in this story as the wood must have been green at the time of which I am writing and Napoleon is known to have had long, strong fingernails.

Another real joy to me in the room is a charming Carlton House desk. A similar desk, although in a better state of preservation, was sold recently at public auction and made over £50,000. An alleged expert looked at mine shortly after the report of the sale had appeared in the press and offered me £25,000. I presume he thought I was a prize sucker and so far I have withstood the many blandishments from would-be purchasers.

In the summer of 1928, I had a large party staying for a Newbury race meeting and amongst them was an American couple I had met in New York.

The wife, who was sleeping in the Herbert bedroom, asked me if I would sell her two small Queen Anne cabinets which were standing in the corridor leading to her bedroom. She offered me $10,000 for them, the dollar at that time was standing at five to the pound.

Her husband had warned her that it would be a great mistake but, nevertheless, whilst assembling for dinner, she broached the subject.

'Dear lady,' I replied, 'I have frequently been approached by intending purchasers as to whether I would sell various items of furniture, silver, china and even pictures. I have always replied in the negative. As I hope to remain in my home for the rest of my days, it would be folly for me to strip the house of the good pieces which adorn it.'

I may refuse to sell my possessions to strangers but I hope I cannot be counted miserly for I was only too happy to give a little silver box to Queen Mary. In common with countless millions of English people, I have the highest regard for our Royal Family, having known many of them from Edward VII and Queen Alexandra onwards.

Queen Mary was a most charming lady. I can still visualize her wearing, as usual, a pale lilac dress with a little toque on her head. I always thought it would make a wonderful nest for some discerning bird to lay its eggs in!

Mabell Airlie, apart from being one of her ladies-in-waiting, was a very close friend of hers. One summer day she telephoned saying, 'My dear Porchey, we are lunching with Frankie de Tuyll not far from Badminton and if you are doing nothing in particular, may we come and have tea with you on our way back to Windsor? There will be three of us, including Tommy Lascelles.'

I told her that would be quite OK and made arrangements for tea to be served in the drawing-room.

After tea, Queen Mary asked me if I would take her to have a look at some of the bedrooms, the library, smoking-room and dining-room. At the time of which I am writing, it was well known to all her many friends that the Queen was in the habit of casting a 'roving eye' on any little *objet d'art* that appealed to her.

When we were in the library, she said to Lady Airlie, 'Mabell, don't you think it's quite remarkable? That dear little box might be a twin of the one I've got in my sitting-room.'

At that stage I suggested that if she would care to accept the 'twin', I would be enchanted for her to have it as a little memento of her visit.

I am often asked if the castle is haunted. Perhaps my father's dabblings in the occult and talk of the Curse of Tutankhamun encourage people to think of Highclere as a spooky place. Personally I don't believe in ghosts and have never considered this castle to be haunted but there are those who have more vivid imaginations than mine. The first account of an apparition occurs in Augustus Hare's autobiography:

Hickledon, December 17 – Mrs George Portal of Burghclere told Charlie Wood that when Allan Herbert was so ill at Highclere – ill to death, it was supposed – the nurse, who was sitting up, saw an old lady come into the room when he was at the worst, gaze at him from the foot of the bed, and nod her head repeatedly. When he was better, and after he could be left, the housekeeper, wishing to give the nurse a little distraction, showed her through the rooms, and in Lord Carnarvon's sitting-room the nurse suddenly pointed at the portrait over the chimney-piece and said, 'That is the lady who came into the sick-room.' The portrait was that of old Lady Carnarvon, Allan Herbert's mother, and the servants well recollected her peculiar way of nodding her head repeatedly.

Stan Anstie, who works for me, is a very level-headed fellow and the last person in the world to be frightened by a ghost yet he told me the following story which took place soon after he had joined the estate maintenance staff and was working at Laundry Cottages. In former days this had been the building where all the laundry from the castle had been taken to be washed and ironed by a bevy of laundrymaids.

The estate carpenter was working on the wide staircase and the rest of the staff were occupied in another part of the building. Suddenly, the carpenter ran through to them, white as a sheet, shaking violently and saying he was never going back there again!

Stan Anstie volunteered to go and collect his tools and whilst he was doing so, he felt something freezing cold brush past him going down the stairs. Being a young man at the time, he took little notice, but when he returned to the others, he found this experience was exactly the same as had happened to the carpenter.

Was this old Lady Carnarvon wandering about? Was it she who also appeared to Hayes and his daughter Pat in 1964 when they were decorating the long passageway that leads from the back door to the cellars and the staircase to the dining-room? This is the oldest part of the castle, the passageway having an arched roof and a stone floor. Leading off it are the butler's office, wine cellars, kitchen and the servants' hall. Next to the servants' hall is a staircase which leads to my study and the centre of the castle.

One evening, Pat was working near the kitchen door and her father was outside the servants' hall, a distance perhaps the length of a cricket pitch. Pat heard her father say 'good evening' to someone and, being puzzled as to who this might be, she turned to look. Seeing no one, she presumed that whoever it was had walked in the opposite direction.

Shortly afterwards, her father accosted her saying he was very angry she had not said 'good evening' to the lady he had seen. He explained that a tall lady, dressed in black, had walked down the stairs from the second floor, going in Pat's direction.

In point of fact, no such person had passed Pat and there was no one on my staff or any guest staying in

the house who bore the slightest resemblance to Mr
Hayes' description of the lady he had seen.

During the war, a woman rushed into the estate office
shouting hysterically, 'I've seen a German.'

My agent, Miss Crystal Stubbings, calmed her
down and acquainted the Home Guard commander of
the situation. Surprisingly, the German was not a
figment of the woman's imagination nor had she seen a
ghost. She had indeed seen a German for one of their
aeroplanes had come down at Woolton Hill and it was
thought that five German airmen were scattered
around the countryside. The Home Guard searched the
woods with tracker dogs and, shortly afterwards, two
airmen were caught.

The Germans dropped a few bombs on my property
but did scant damage. They seemed to think that the
lime kilns at Burghclere were an arms dump and on
one occasion dropped a stick of twelve Molotov cock-
tails. There were many other incidents and bombs
were dropped on the Home Guard hut at Siddown Hill
which was on fire so the German pilot seemed to think
that it was a legitimate target. He let fly his bombs
which sucked the leaded windows out of the castle.

Despite these depredations, little has changed outside over the years. My paddocks and the golf course
were ploughed up to produce crops during the war and
a great deal of timber was cut but the mighty cedars of
Lebanon still flourish.

After the war I started a great re-afforestation
scheme to make good all the losses, for I have always

taken much pleasure in forestry, and from the moment I succeeded to this place, I have cherished the woodland. What does annoy me however is to be told *ad nauseum* how dreadful it would be if such and such a tree were to be felled. From long experience I have found that very often it greatly improves the scenery if trees which are old and liable to be blown down are removed. Like everybody else, of course, I deplore the loss of an exotic old cedar which has taken over three hundred years to grow to its full stature. But it is a waste of time to pine over rotten timber which can be replaced. Replanting is the only way by which we can ensure the future of our forests. Most of my readers would agree with me if they could see the young plantations when they change colour in spring and autumn and more than compensate for the loss of the old favourites which have long passed their prime.

6
Twixt Top and Bottom

WHEN I INHERITED I found, to my horror, that all the lovely oak in the saloon was covered with about one-eighth of an inch of orange varnish and the stonework had all been painted Chinese white. I had not given it much thought before this as I had been away from home so much. I arranged to have this paint and varnish removed and asked my sister if she would supervise the work while I was abroad. She was good enough to do this and the natural oak was revealed in all its pristine glory and the saloon returned to its original state. She also refurnished most of the bedrooms, putting in several new bathrooms and spent, at my insistence, quite a lot of cash on the dining-room, library and smoking-room as well as my study and my wife's boudoir.

It may amuse my readers to know that in the year 1923, there were eighteen domestic servants employed in the castle. There was my father's valet, a charming man called George Fearnside, my mother's maid, Streatfield the butler, the groom of the chambers, three footmen, a stewards' room boy who looked after the staff, four in the kitchen, Mrs Maclean, the Scottish housekeeper, four housemaids and a night-watchman

Stratford by name but commonly known as Creeping Jesus.

It was the custom in those days that if there were more than ten for dinner, the footmen wore knee-breeches and powdered their hair. Not long after I succeeded, the footmen lined up and said they were sorry but they could no longer continue to powder their hair as the glycerine and powder took too long to wash out. I agreed, as I felt those days were over. I also told them that I was afraid some of them would have to go as I could no longer afford to keep them all. It was a sad day for me but most of them found jobs with friends of mine, so consequently, no great hardship was suffered.

Even when the slump occurred in 1931, I did not stint my guests when they came to cheer me up even though I had to change my pattern of life, to economize and to try to consume considerably less food and wine when I was alone.

In company with thousands of others I suddenly woke up to the fact that my securities and properties were worth about one quarter of what they had been valued at a year previously. There were a great many suicides among those unfortunates who had been completely ruined and it is said that when a man booked a hotel room on the top floor in New York he was asked if he wanted it for sleeping or jumping.

Despite making economies, I was still able to entertain in style during the shooting season and for Newbury races. The number of people employed about the castle were fewer than in my father's day but I liked to think that the standard of hospitality was just as high.

Highclere Castle.

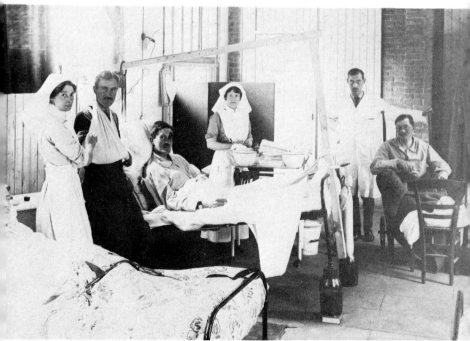

During the First World War Highclere was used as a hospital for wounded officers.

Lord Carnarvon and his first wife, Catherine (*left*), on the second day at Ascot in June 1924.

On the fourth day at Ascot, 1924.

Lord Carnarvon, all smiles, after riding Claudine, the winner of the Southdown Welter Handicap Plate, 1933.

His children, Lady Penelope Herbert and Lord Porchester, in the Red Bug.

With Cardy Montagu at a barbecue in Nassau, 1939.

A drive at Highclere.
During the Second World War.

With Deanna Durbin in 1947.

In Hollywood on the set of *The Four Feathers* with Claudette
Colbert and Victor McLaghlen.

ABOVE: With Harold Macmillan.

BELOW: At Highclere with Sir Alec Douglas Home (*right*).

Outside Highclere Castle.

I have always made a point of knowing my employees and have kept a close personal relationship with most of them. I've taken care to see that they were happy and well-fed and able to enjoy themselves after their work. Readers may feel that this is wishful thinking on my part for today people seem to imagine that working in a great house in the olden days was akin to slavery. But when *No Regrets* was published I received many letters, and several of them were from old retainers, whom I remember well.

A typical one said: 'As one of your very old and faithful servants ... I think I spent ten of the happiest and most memorable years of my life at Highclere Castle.'

Readers may still remain sceptical and think that such sentiments are few and far between. This makes me sad. I would like to convince all my readers that a great house was a friendly, lively and cheerful place to live whether you were upstairs or downstairs. I cannot quote from all the letters I received so instead I offer some excerpts from Mrs Hart, who has most kindly given me permission to publish the following:

My mother saw an advertisement in the paper through a Registry Office in London. It was one of my first railway trips on my own and Highclere was a difficult place to get to. I wasn't very old so I was pleased to see someone waiting to meet me at Newbury, with a little motor van.

I arrived and the housekeeper showed me into this lovely little sitting-room. I felt quite at home. She was a very tall dark woman, North country I think. She asked me my name and I said Matilda, but that half the family called me Tilda and the other half Tillie, so she said that she thought with all the men servants about it'd better be shortened to Mattie.

She was very kind to us girls. After I had had a meal she showed me over the castle. I was frightened, it was so big and all those big corridors. I thought I'd never be able to work there. However I was put as fourth maid and given my little jobs to do. Next morning I started off cleaning the housekeeper's bedroom. As I was doing the grate, I turned the carpet back and I thought my goodness me, there was as much coal under the carpet as there was in the fire. The other girl said you'll never get round if you fuss like that and I said oh yes I will. So I cleared it all up – I had nearly half a bag of coal from under the carpet. After I got that done, things seemed to fall into place. It's funny, when there is an army of people it's all organized very well. I can remember the head housemaid, she was very nice, she used to feed with us in the little sitting-room, we used to have our breakfast in there, the little room into the left when you go in the back door. We got up fairly early and had a cup of tea and then off we went – my job was the grates – and one of the grates that I had to do was the pink room. Is there still all the brass – the poker, shovel? A lovely basket grate? It was all beautiful and I had to polish the brass every day. The curtains were pink brocade – I've never seen anything so lovely. You had to be very careful, there was a big cord to pull them with. Your feet sunk in the carpet – it was pink too. Then I got on my knees and swept the carpet over with the dustpan and brush then the head housemaid would come in with her gloves on to do the dusting. That would make marks in the carpet and she would call you and you just took the marks off the carpet. First thing in the morning was when his lordship had one of these wooden things with your head out – a Turkish bath – and there was a fireplace in there. Only once it let me down and I was called back to do it. I don't know if they do it now but then the fires were done with pure white paper folded up in a certain way with the corners turned back and that would fit round the grate perfectly. No newspapers, it had to be pure white paper that was used. That was how we laid the fires. All the fireplaces were the same.

After everything was done, the footman came along with the coal and lit the fires. We worked up a pattern, when we'd finished our rounds in the morning we'd go down to our little sitting-room and have breakfast. Now, this to me was like a dinner because we were waited on by a boy called John. From the kitchen would come a big dish laden with lovely bacon and kidneys, toast, marmalade and butter. Then the four or five of us girls would tuck in.

The rest of the morning before lunch we had all the beds to make and the bedrooms to do. Betty and I used to do the boys' rooms and make all the beds for the visiting valets. It was a back-breaking job, one after another. But everything was very well organized and all worked like a machine.

We'd have our lunch in the servants' hall. There was a long table which was oak and long forms and an oak floor. There was a lovely fire in there too. All the boys would sit down one side and all the girls down the other. Frank the head footman sat at the head of the table and woe betide you if you had your sleeves turned up. Frank used to stand there with the carving knife and there would be a beautiful big joint. We had wonderful food. We used to laugh at the girl who sat next to me as she couldn't eat prunes and junket because it made her tummy gurgle. The butler and the housekeeper had their meals in the steward's room. I think the cook had hers in there too but I never was in that room. There were places you never went. I never went in the kitchen.

After lunch we could go up, have a bath, do our rooms and then down into the sitting-room for tea. If you filled the bath up you more or less swam in it. After tea there was a bit of a scurry again because if there were a lot of people staying, there was much to be done. White cans full of hot water had to be stood in all the bedrooms with towels over them and all the beds turned down. There was a special way to do it with the crest showing on the beautiful linen sheets. Then you raced downstairs again whilst they were all in their bedrooms getting ready to come down to dinner and chased through the ground floor rooms, plumping cushions, emptying ashtrays, tidying grates and making up fires. You used to do that quickly, taking care to wipe your footsteps off the carpet. It was all done fast and simply by careful planning.

Then in the evening we used to have a hot supper in the servants' hall. Beautiful food. If it had been a big joint at lunch, you might have it done in some way for supper but you never saw it again. The food was as good as in the dining-room.

After supper and after they'd finished their dinner, and we had finished our duties, we could go down into the hall and that was where I learnt to dance. 'Three o'clock in the Morning' I remember was a popular tune. We had fun down there. Then we used to go back to our rooms and the head housemaid had a wonderful way of making cocoa. I can see her now standing in front of the fire. She gave us all a cup of cocoa before we went to bed.

Lord Porchester was actually born when I was there. We were all assembled outside his lordship's room and we went in one at a time. When your name was called, you went in, did a little curtsy, held your hand out and a golden sovereign was put in it with a few words that it was in honour of his son and heir and you said, 'Thank you, m'lord', did your curtsy and came out. We all had to have lovely clean aprons.

I often think to myself what a stupid thing I did with the money. My father was very angry when I told him. We all pooled together and we bought this silly little gramophone. It folded up, a cylinder sort of thing. When we split up I don't know what happened to it or who had it. But we did get a lot of pleasure out of it.

Us three girls were all about the same age and we were put to sleep together in a very big room in the front of the castle. Betty was full of beans, the life and soul of the party, well, you had to have some fun, couldn't have all work and no play but sometimes we were a bit noisy so we were put up into this big tower where we had a bedroom each. Betty used to play our little gramophone under the sheets.

Nanny complained, she was sure she could hear music and it frightened her in the night so, of course, that had to stop.

Then we were parted, one on one side of the tower and one on the other. Betty had no fear, no fear at all, and one night I heard a tap, tap, tap on the window. She had walked along the lead guttering. We all did it in the end. I was terrified but I did it. The next thing was Nanny said she was sure she could hear people walking about on the roof.

Although it was such a big castle, it was never cold. We were allowed to have fires in our bedrooms but you had to keep the fireguard there. The coal used to come up on a lift. If I had to earn my living, I'd do it all again. I'll never forget it, it was so well organized and so lovely.

Sometimes everyone would be away for quite a while and you could get on with all the jobs that you had had to neglect. When everyone was away, the caretakers used to allow Frank to take the boats out on the lake and Frank taught me to row. He was a very gentlemanly person and I felt safe and happy with him.

Another picture of Highclere during this period can be gained from Mr Day's reminiscences. He joined us as estate electrician in the days when we made our own electricity and has stayed with us ever since although of course we are now on the mains. A pillar of our local community, Mr Day has been churchwarden here for thirty years now and in 1979 he had the honour of being chosen to receive Maundy Money from the Queen in Winchester Cathedral. Mr Day wrote to me:

I came to Highclere Castle not long after Lady Penelope was christened. I remember her being taken to church in a pony and trap. The family came in their Rolls Royce which was off-white with red wheels and had the family crest on the doors. On one occasion two little boys were discovered carefully picking the crest off one of the doors. The baby's pram was also off-white with red wheels.

When Lord Porchester was about six years old, his father bought him an electric car which the family soon named 'The Red Bug', because it too was painted in the family colours with its wheels picked out in red. When it arrived, Lord Carnarvon and his brother-in-law Sir Brograve Beauchámp were the first to try it. When Lord Porchester wanted to drive it the battery had run down and, to his great disappointment, he had to wait until the following day when I had managed to recharge the battery.

On another occasion I remember when Lord Porchester and his sister Lady Penelope were children, a marvellous fancy-dress party was held in the castle. Everything was decorated in silver and white, including the costumes which the children wore.

In those days, when we were not working, we played billiards and cards. The groom and valet were ex-service men and it was quite usual to see a four-and-a-half gallon of beer finished in less than a week. They started the day at six o'clock with a pint and a cigarette and finished it in the same way.

At Christmas there was a staff dance which took place in the library and the staffs of other houses in the locality were invited. As these dances finished very late and the housemaids had to rise very early in the morning, they usually missed out on their night's sleep.

Some idea of life at Highclere forty years ago can be gained from a list of the annual salaries received by the various members of my staff in 1939. I cannot remember what the head gardener, head forester, stud groom or other senior outside employees received but I have listed below some of the others to give an idea of staff hierarchy:

Chef	£260
Head chauffeur	188
Electrician	182
Butler	132
Head groom	130
Second chauffeur	117
Second groom	110
Third groom	104
Housekeeper	100
First footman	80
Valet	80
Usher (not living in)	78
First housemaid	65
Nightwatchman	65
Stable cook	65
First kitchenmaid	60
Second footman	54
Second kitchenmaid	48
Second housemaid	48
Third housemaid	40
Fourth housemaid	38
Hall boy	30
Scullery maid	30

Robert Taylor, my butler, has now been with me for forty-four years. He joined me on the evening of 29 February 1936 to become first footman. Describing his arrival, he said:

Mr Smith, the butler, made me very welcome when we met and told me to come down to the staff hall after I had unpacked and settled in. The following morning I was shown round the house by Mr Smith. I remember being greatly impressed with the drawing-room and its beautiful peacock overlay carpet. At that time the house seemed huge – now it has shrunk with the years. We continued our tour and, in the silver room, Mr Smith explained when the various services were used; the Bretbury for dinner and the Chesterfield for luncheon. As we left, he handed me the key, saying, 'The silver will be your responsibility from now on.'

I was to find out in time that a considerable amount of entertaining was done and on these occasions we worked very long hours but this was compensated for by his lordship's frequent absences from the castle. From the staff point of view, Highclere was a happy household although strict discipline was maintained by the butler and Mrs Saunderson, the housekeeper. Once a fortnight the second chauffeur was detailed to take the staff to the local dances but if we wanted to go at any other time, we had to ask the butler's permission. Every Tuesday and Thursday, the staff bus took those of us who were off duty to Newbury, leaving the castle at 2.00 pm and returning at 6.00 pm. During Ascot week, the staff bus took us all for a day at the races.

The men on the staff, indoor and outdoor, had a clubroom in the stable yard where they could play billiards and darts. We also had our own cricket team, playing mid-week matches against teams from other estates, and the home match teas were provided by his lordship. This, perhaps, gives some idea of the comradeship which existed amongst the staff in those days.

However, the highlight of the year was our staff dance when we were allowed to invite staff from the other houses in the neighbourhood. Dancing took place in the library and the chef provided excellent refreshments. We, in turn, were invited to dances at Sir Frederick Carden's home, Stargroves, Lady Benson's at Twyford and at the home of Mr and Mrs Elliot-Cohen.

There were very few changes in the domestic staff and life proceeded in this way until war broke out in September 1939. A few months later, his lordship's valet left and I was asked to take over his duties. Then Mr Smith had a recurrence of a previous illness which necessitated him giving up private service for an outdoor job and he was succeeded by Mr Pell. In January 1940 his lordship rejoined his regiment and I went with him as his army servant. This was short lived as these jobs were taken over by Grade C3 personnel and I was transferred to the Royal Armoured Corps on active duty. My place as soldier-servant was taken by Trooper Bloss.

Most people's servants were called up when the war started. Several of mine had joined the army soon after hostilities began and I was left with an elderly man, Mr Pell, as my butler. Pell had been my friend Murray Graham's servant before he retired but he had kindly offered to give up his retirement for the moment and come to Highclere to help me out for the duration of the war. However there was a great deal of work for him to do so I knew he would be glad of assistance, should I be able to find someone.

One night I was staying at the Ritz and found myself being valeted by a well-spoken chap with a very pleasing personality. I asked him if he received a good wage from the hotel and he replied that it was small but that he usually earned quite an appreciable sum in tips and, as a result, was able to maintain a nice little flat in town. However he said he would be happy to come to Highclere to help Mr Pell.

He duly came to Highclere and proved a great success until one weekend in the summer of 1943 when Bobby Throckmorton and his wife were spending the weekend with me. Unfortunately Bobby recognized him, as he had been his Uncle Basil's servant in Windsor. Bobby told me that he had stolen a great deal of his uncle's jewellery and silver and that the police had been looking for him for the last three years.

Bobby insisted on telephoning the Windsor police and I arranged that our local police should be informed simultaneously. Realizing he had been recognized by Bobby, he decided to pack his bag and make a hasty departure, helping himself to some cuff-links and tie pins which he thought would make a nice souvenir of his sojourn with me. Unfortunately for him, he was arrested by our local policeman as he was leaving the castle.

Shortly afterwards, I received the following letter from Oxford Prison:

My Lord, I need hardly tell you that I fear I shall be His Majesty's guest for a considerable time. I was so happy at Highclere and wish to thank your lordship for all the kindness I received while in your service. I felt particularly upset at having to leave so hurriedly when I knew that Mr Pell would have to cope with a lot of work due to my sudden departure.

As well as Mr Pell and his unfortunate assistant during the war, I had as my soldier-servant, Trooper Bloss, who had been recommended to me by my friend Puggy Howes. Puggy said that Bloss was a good chap who had been at Lord Scarbrough's, where he was married to the head housemaid. Bloss had joined the Yorkshire Dragoons but he was found unfit for service abroad as he had varicose veins.

Bloss duly presented himself at my office in Winchester and I explained what it was I would want him to do. 'Righto,' he said, 'I'll do my best.' And so I was left to the tender mercies of Arthur Bloss.

He was a good driver and looked after me well but I quickly found out that he was the cleverest scrounger that ever lived. One day he told me he had found a little village about six miles away and the butcher there had told him that if he wanted anything for his lordship, just to let him know. A leg of lamb or whatever was wanted could be put in the back of a car with a blanket over it and taken to Highclere.

'In return', said Bloss, 'they would like perhaps half a dozen pheasants, a few rabbits and perhaps some hares. Just leave it to me.' It worked like a charm.

One day I had to go to Devizes and we had been motoring for some time and poor old Bloss had clearly lost his way.

'For God's sake,' I said irritably, 'you are the stupidest man I've ever known. You must have taken the wrong road for we are going round in circles. Look at the map.'

Bloss replied, 'Now look m'lord, it's no good getting excited. You'll only catch a cold and if you catch a cold you'll be laid up. If you are laid up there will be doctors' bills and God knows what to pay and we shall be out of action.' He continued in his Yorkshire accent, 'Now if I had your brains, instead of being a trooper I might even be a colonel like you. So don't get annoyed with me. If you know the way to Devizes, why don't you tell me?'

Bloss was a very kindly man who adored children. He used to take my son fishing and also take my daughter Penelope out whenever she was at home. He was much beloved too by the evacuee children who inhabited the castle during the war. He told me that one of these children always referred to me as King Carnarvon for he said that only a king could live in a castle.

When Bloss and I came back to Highclere for weekends, as you can imagine, he was *persona grata* in the kitchen, where he supplemented our rations, which in those days were meagre, with his intensely clever efforts locally.

When my headquarters were in Salisbury, we used to stay in Sammy Christie-Miller's house, and his dear old mother and his sister Veronica used to ask me to go out and shoot whatever I could find on their estate. Whenever I had a couple of hours to spare of an afternoon, I would go out after pheasant, rabbit, hare and pigeon for the larder. The head gamekeeper was still there, a sweet old boy, three or four farmhands would come as beaters and Bloss would act as my loader. We stood at the end of one of this estate's long belts of trees whilst partridge or woodcock were driven over us. I normally got quite a bag and dear old Mrs Christie-Miller was delighted because it helped to supplement the rations.

Bloss was however a perfectly appalling loader for he would stand there gazing around him, talking away and quite forget to load my gun. My bold Bloss was far too interested and voluble about everything about him, he would say: 'By gum, you got two there, a right and a left, two cocks.'

I'd say: 'No, a cock and a hen, doesn't matter, give me a gun.'

'Oh aye', he'd say, 'I'd forgotten about that, here you are, I've loaded it.'

'You bloody fool, you'd have made an awful mistake if you hadn't.'

Then we'd carry on with the day's sport as best we could.

Trooper Bloss, with his ingenious and fertile brain came to the conclusion that my car, which was a camouflaged Vauxhall and looked like a military

vehicle, should have a little red and blue flag instead of
the racing mascot which was usually on it. He said it
would look like a general's pennant, so I said all right,
as it was a civilian car with a civilian registration
number. So he got one of these beautiful flags fixed up
on the front of the car.

It was quite remarkable. Large convoys of troops
lurched to the side of the road, military policemen
sprang to attention and saluted for they thought I was
some high-ranking officer of great importance.
Everybody moved out of the way and so we got clear
runs all over the place, which was quite an asset in those
difficult times.

Usually I took a sandwich lunch with me and a
thermos of coffee and we kept warm as best we could
and got on with our job. Southern Command was a big
area and there were times when we had long journeys
to make. On one occasion we were returning from
Devizes when all of a sudden, I couldn't believe my
eyes, there must have been ten thousand rats crossing
the road in front of us. A solid phalanx of rats, it
seemed unending. We pulled up.

'I've never seen anything like that, I can't bear it,' I
said to Bloss.

'Why don't we drive straight through the boogers,
at least we'll squash some of them, won't we, colonel?'
Bloss replied in his broad Yorkshire accent.

'I suppose so, but what if some of the beastly things
leap up on the car?'

'I'll shut my windows and you shut yours and they
can't get in to us then. I'll put on my headlights and I'll
drive straight through, OK?'

Actually, I shut my eyes because I cannot bear

anything of that sort. There were horrid squeaks and groans but we were soon through.

Funnily enough, a lot of people in the neighbour-hood witnessed this extraordinary migration of rats but to this day no one knows how or why it occurred. Probably they had organized between themselves to march away from x which had upset them to y where they thought they could get food. That was the only explanation anyone could think of.

It was quite a shock when one day, towards the end of the war, Bloss came to me and said: 'I've very bad news.'

'What's happened?' I replied.

'Well, it's about the wife.'

'Oh dear, I hope...'

'No, no,' he said, 'nothing like that ... blow me down if the wife hasn't had a legacy of £20,000. Now this is what is worrying me. She says in her letter that now she has the money she is determined to buy a cottage she's been after for a long time and she says I have to go back and help her. I was looking forward to bringing the wife to Highclere because I love working for you and I like the people here and I don't like the idea of going back to Yorkshire but what can I do?'

'Dear Bloss,' I said, 'you're married to the lady so I don't see what else you can do. It's Hobson's choice. But I don't want to feel responsible for breaking up a happy home so I think you'd better go.'

So, alas, he departed, which left me sad. He had been a great stop-gap. Poor Robert Taylor had been badly wounded in the invasion of Normandy. He was the only one left alive in his tank but I am happy to say that I soon got news of him when he was taken to Derby General Hospital and after a bit he fully recovered and was able to return to me at Highclere. Jack Gibbins, who used to be my chauffeur, drove King George VI during the war and I am glad to say he is well and has a garage near the castle today.

The number of staff at Highclere has decreased steadily over the years but I hope that my guests still find my hospitality adequate. I have always taken a great interest in eating and drinking and in my house I have the best possible food and wine. If the host gives it his personal attention, an atmosphere is engendered wherein guests are relaxed and happy. I have a superb cook and this makes me the envy of many of my friends. Perhaps it is the French blood in my veins which accounts for my understanding and love of good living.

In so many houses, the host and hostess seem to be quite indifferent. I remember once staying with one of the richest men in the country and I thought the food was very moderate. I told my host what I felt about this matter and was horrified to learn that he considered food was just petrol. I told him that I bought the best petrol for my car as I considered it would go better on top quality fuel!

Today at Highclere I have a tiny little staff. Robert Taylor is still with me after forty-four years. He is acclaimed, by common consent, as the greatest living example of the perfect butler. I would not be able to run this place without his invaluable help. Presiding in the kitchen is my beloved cook, Ivy Rogers. Missen, my chauffeur, has been with me over twenty years and his wife, Julie, helps in the kitchen. Lastly, my house-keeper, Mrs Reid, to whom I am devoted. She is as irreplaceable as the others I have mentioned. I have to be very careful and sparing of these unique people because they are the lynchpin of this establishment which is probably one of the last links of the feudal system. We are all part of one big family and share in each other's joys and sorrows.

7
French Frolics

The last time I saw Paris,
Her heart was warm and gay,
No matter how they change her
I'll remember her that way.

I HAVE TRAVELLED a great deal and am sometimes
asked which country I have most enjoyed visiting. I
must confess that the answer would have to be France
because it is unique. The cooking is so good and I love
the atmosphere. There is a gaiety about France which is
infectious and Paris is a wonderful city which I enjoy
more and more.

When I was young, I often went over to Paris and
normally stayed at the Ritz. It was then – and still is –
the nicest hotel in the world as the location is charming
and I usually see masses of friends there.

At the time about which I am writing, Claude
Auzello was managing director. He was one of the
most dedicated hoteliers I have ever known, always
beautifully dressed and devoted to his job. He got on
well with old Charlie Ritz who owned the place, Charlie being a bachelor and nephew of César Ritz, who
built the hotel.

Claude's wife, Blanche, was a very pretty Jewess whose name was Rubenstein but, after the outbreak of hostilities, she had it changed to Ross. Claude married her when she was young and beautiful although at that time reputedly having affairs with various men. She had been the mistress of a rich Egyptian who professed to be in the film business. Before her marriage to Claude, Blanche had hopes of becoming an actress and her lover wanted to take her to Egypt to star in a film he was producing. Despite all his blandishments, she refused to go and married Claude who was madly in love with her.

During the German occupation, General von Stulp-nagel, who was Military Governor of Paris, moved into the Ritz with his staff. He was unusually friendly and wanted the hotel to continue functioning as normally as possible. With his goodwill and help, this hope was realized to some extent.

Blanche was a brave woman who loved France. By chance she came in contact with a Polish girl who was working for the French Resistance. This girl asked Blanche to find her a hiding place as the Germans were searching for her. Blanche did so although she knew full well that she was placing her husband and herself in great danger. Eventually, the Polish agent was caught while transmitting a wireless message to England. To the distress of all who knew her, she was tortured and executed by the Nazis. Claude, who had won the Legion of Honour and other decorations in the First World War, was so concerned about his wife's safety that he forbade her to have anything more to do with the resistance movement.

During the war, I heard from American friends that

Walter Winchell and Elsa Maxwell, neither of whom liked Blanche, had concocted some yarn which was published in their syndicated column stating that Blanche had been executed by the Nazis. They also wrote at that time that Coco Chanel, as well as Ruth and André Dubonnet were in serious trouble with the Germans. All these tales were quite untrue.

After the war ended, Claude Auzello became very depressed and showed suicidal tendencies. To the great sorrow of his many friends, he shot his wife and then turned the revolver on himself – a tragic end to the lives of two brave people.

A very nice Polish gentleman, Mr Zambruski, succeeded Auzello as managing director, a position which he filled admirably until his retirement.

Paris is my favourite of all the European capitals but, sadly, I now go rarely to that lovely city in which I had such fun for so long. She is indestructible and, I trust, immortal.

Before the Second World War, I often stayed in the South of France with Eddy, grandfather of the present Lord Derby. Lord Stanley's wife, Portia, was a most entertaining lady and she and I were great friends. I well understood her foibles.

Eddy used to invite me regularly to spend a fortnight in the winter at Sansovino which was a delightful house he owned in Cannes, very near to the golf course at Mougins. He was the big shot there as he had more or less designed the golf course to suit his own tastes. It was a very nice course at that time and we used to lunch there most days after playing eighteen holes in the morning. Unfortunately, I have not played there for a great many years.

Sansovino epitomized gracious living and old world charm. For instance, at about six o'clock most evenings, Ellis, the butler, would announce, 'His lordship is ready to receive you in his bedroom.'

This summons was called the *levée du roi* and Eddy, sitting up in bed in great good spirits, ate caviare sandwiches, drank champagne and insisted that we should regale ourselves in like manner. There were usually about half a dozen of us there and I was always called upon to do some of my famous imitations. This performance amused Eddy hugely and he used to shake with laughter and say, 'Oh, Porchey, I did love that, please do some others.'

Later in the evening we went to the casino where I was made to sit behind Lady Stanley while she was playing baccarat as she insisted that I brought her luck.

Zographos, the Greek banker, was a great character whom I liked immensely. He always kept his cool and on the rare occasion that he had a losing run, he took it in his stride. He told me never to play as I was not a gambler and never would be. How right he was! He said, 'You put on a little money in fear and trembling and, if you win, instead of leaving it on at least twice more, you snatch it off and sit back on your seat looking as if you had just had a tooth extracted.'

I became a member of the Travellers' Club in Paris in 1928; it was a lovely building in the Avenue des Champs Elysées.

One evening I was playing bridge before dinner and, having won several rubbers, I went to watch another table where a French friend was playing. He had told me that a man who was playing at the same table usually won and my pal was convinced that he did so by cheating. Although he had watched him closely for a considerable time, he had been unable to discover the method employed.

On this particular evening, while I was watching, my friend suddenly leapt to his feet and shouted that he had caught him red-handed. He then described the method used.

'When it is his turn to shuffle, he does it so quickly that he is able to slip an ace with another card in between another ace and, after dealing, should he have neither of these aces, he knows they are held by his opponents.'

This gave him a very big edge and when he was denounced so vigorously, the gentleman in question rose from his seat and stole silently away.

I learnt shortly afterwards that he walked straight to the accountant's desk, presented his bridge card which showed him to be a winner that evening and asked how much he was in credit. The accountant replied that he would go upstairs and check because he thought it was a very substantial sum. The swindler asked him to bring back a cheque for the whole amount which, luckily for him, the accountant was able to do as the secretary was in his office upstairs and only he was able to sign cheques.

'Thank you very much,' said the culprit, 'I'm most grateful.'

He presented the cheque to his bank early next

morning and asked that it should be cleared immediately as he was going for a holiday.

I need hardly add that he was kicked out of the
Travellers' Club. Had my friend not caught him out,
he might well have got away with the trick for years.

I still go to Deauville for a fortnight's holiday each
summer. The stud farms are of tremendous interest to
me, the golf course is always a joy and I have so many
friends living in that part of France that I am never at a
loss for company. When I am in Deauville, I usually
stay at the Hôtel Royale for the good reason that Monsieur Mouchet, a most charming man, runs his establishment superbly. There is a little club just across the
road from the hotel which only opens for the month of
August, I pop in there to eat delicious meals with old
friends who have also come over for the racing and the
sales.

I also visit Le Touquet which has an excellent golf
course. I won the Portland Handicap Golf Tournament
there one year and was runner-up on another occasion.
In 1977 I failed to qualify for the tournament itself but
won the second flight for which I received a magnificent gift of two jeroboams of Bollinger 1969 champagne.

Playing in golf tournaments is always good fun
whether at Le Touquet or elsewhere. I try hard but
seldom succeed. On one occasion I remember being in
the final of a tournament at Swinley in Berkshire. At
the sixteenth hole I was still one up but in the rough.
My caddy said, 'Now m'lord, you take your mashy

niblick, keep your head down, swing through and you'll be on the green.'

I had one hell of a swipe, topped the ball and sent it sailing far over the green. Quentin Hoare and I dead-heated at the seventeenth, so the eighteenth was crucial. My drive wasn't too bad and I was up on the green in two. Then the tension proved too great: I mucked my putt and lost.

Indeed I play more golf nowadays than I ever did, for it is a leisurely game more suited to an octogenarian than the equestrian pursuits that occupied me when I was young, when I used to hunt, ride in races and play polo.

I first learnt golf on our own course at Highclere. My father employed a dear old professional called Ben Sayers to design and lay out a charming little nine-hole course. When I succeeded in 1923, I had it enlarged by another nine holes. During the war it was ploughed up for food production. I never replaced it but I continue to play golf.

It's a good game for you can play it all over the world, it enables you to meet interesting people, and you can talk to them as you walk from hole to hole. In Palm Springs, California, I had many happy games with Bob Hope and Bing Crosby. They were fun to play either with or against as they ragged each other and told lovely stories: the whole thing was a joy.

A publisher I was talking to in the United States asked me to guess which was the most popular game in America. I said baseball. I was wrong so I tried again and suggested tennis, or perhaps American football, but no, golf is the most popular game.

One of the strangest courses I ever played on was in

Egypt at Gezireh. The course was perfectly flat and having played a rather good drive straight down the middle, I was horrified to see a large bird called a kite descend on the ball and remove it. My caddy told me this was not uncommon but that the bird usually placed the ball on top of a palm tree and that was the last one saw of it. Exactly that happened to me but the local rules were such that you placed another ball in position and carried on with the game.

I suppose my most historic game was with the Duke of Windsor when he was Prince of Wales and courting Wallis Simpson. It was just before their epic cruise in the *Nahlin* along the Balkan coast which had such disastrous repercussions. We played on the Venice Lido with his friend Eric Dudley and had a splendid lunch in the middle, which was full of talk and laughter; we were oblivious of what was to come.

8
Voyages East

I HAVE BEEN to many places all over the globe, too many to mention specifically and I am glad to say that I enjoyed visiting most of them. In particular some of my trips to the Far East remain etched in my memory.

Florence Desmond and her husband Charles asked me to accompany them on a trip which started off at Beirut and then continued to Singapore and Hong Kong.

Beirut was a beautiful town and I am glad to have seen it before it was completely destroyed. Funnily enough only six months ago in London, I ran into one of the leading lights of Beirut, with whom I had played golf on this trip. He told me that the only thing that had escaped in the recent general confusion of the fighting was the golf course, which is so far unscathed.

After a few days in Beirut, wining and dining and meeting all the local bigwigs, we flew on to Singapore where we stayed in the greatest luxury. The racecourse was excellent and we were wonderfully entertained by all manner of dignitaries. I was treated as if I were the personification of the greatest VIP of all time, thoroughly spoiled and I enjoyed every minute of it.

The culmination of our visit was to be invited to lunch by the aged but charming Sultan of Johore. He gave a splendid party for us. The food was disgusting but that didn't matter as the old boy spoke very good English, was a delight to talk to, a great anglophile and had asked cheery friends.

After lunch the Sultan suggested to 'Desi' Hughes-don that it might amuse her to see his priceless collection of jewels which were kept in an enormous Chubb safe, as big as a small room, which reposed in his bedroom. The safe had heavy doors which you could not have blasted with dynamite and a secret combination lock of which only he and one other had the key. The safe was concealed in a huge cupboard, with his shirts and ties hanging in front so that anyone entering the room would imagine it to be but an extra large dressing-room.

His jewels were one of the most fabulous collections of precious stones I have ever set eyes on. We were told to sit down, His Highness opened his treasure trove, and started passing round the beautiful pieces. Nobody had the slightest chance of purloining any of the rings for an officer of the Sultan's bodyguard watched over the proceedings with the eyes of a hawk!

The Sultan had a private army of about eight hundred officers and men who were a very smart lot and kept a close watch on everything concerning the Sultan's welfare. This particular officer stood there and his eyes never left the different pieces as they were handed round and admired. He took them himself from the last person and laid them carefully on a table, then they were put back inside the safe. I wondered if he had had any rough customers around before we had arrived.

The finest stone of all, to my mind, was the most enormous, absolutely marvellous emerald, weighing something like fifty carats and square cut. I know quite a bit about stones and one of this emerald's rare qualities was that there was no silk in it. I was given a magnifying glass and as I peered down at the stone, I felt that it was certainly one of the best I'd ever see!

The Sultan was very proud of it but he had other lovely gems, blood red rubies, sapphires, rows of huge ornamental pieces dating from his father's time, much modern jewellery and some magnificent diamonds purchased for him by Harry Winston in New York. His Highness considered his finest possession to be a unique rope of matching pearls which put round your neck would have reached to your thighs. Those at the beginning were the size of peas and they graded up to ones the size of marbles.

You can always tell the difference between an artificial pearl and a real one because the genuine one feels rough if you rub it against your tooth. They have never succeeded in making an artificial one gritty. I couldn't resist rubbing one of these marvellous marbles against my tooth. Everyone laughed at this for it looked as if I was not sure whether they were real or not.

The Sultan then asked me if I liked shooting and when I said I did, he took me into his gun room and showed me at least four pairs of magnificent Purdey's. He also had some beautifully balanced revolvers, some very fine automatics and masses of ammunition. He told me that I was very welcome to take an automatic away with me but I declined as I was going on to Hong Kong and did not know what the police would say if I arrived with one. I hoped that it would be unlikely that I would ever need to draw a gun on anyone.

Hong Kong was teeming with human beings. I didn't think I'd ever seen so many before, all so busy but so many on the breadline. Enormous wealth contrasted with great poverty – unbelievable really.

I discovered to my delight that I could have a pair of Maxwell shoes copied in two days. The man came along to my hotel, measured my foot, asked me if he could take away one of my own shoes for a short time and returned in two days with a perfectly splendid pair in good leather, most comfortable – I could hardly tell the difference. The great Maxwell of Bond Street now takes eighteen months to two years to make a pair and charges £180.

The same went for a suit of clothes. I had a superbly tailored suit made in English cloth for £15 in forty-eight hours.

In the old days Hong Kong had but one race-course, called Happy Valley. Sir Douglas Clague was the big-shot and there was a huge luncheon room. Whilst you ate, the waiters came round and showed you a list of prices, if you wanted to bet they would place it for you and come back with the ticket; if the horse won they would collect your winnings for you because betting was illegal except for the tote, although there were a few illicit bookmakers. Now there is a brand new,

all-weather race-course open in Hong Kong, called
Shatin, but I have yet to see it in action.

After enjoying myself in the company of Frankie More
O'Ferrall, I went on to the Philippines and to Honolulu
where the pineapples grow. Patrick Beresford was
playing polo so I watched him when I wasn't playing
golf. Meanwhile Florence Desmond's husband,
Charles, had gone on to Australia. I ended up at the
Beverly Hills Hotel and hereby hangs a tale.

Frankie More O'Ferrall was great friends with Bing
Crosby and so was I. Bing rang us up and said, 'I've a
two-year-old which hasn't grown much but it is by
Bold Lad.'

Bold Lad stood at Frankie's brother's stud so he
listened hard.

'It's a nice little brown colt and I'd love you and
Porchey to buy it if you like it. It's not expensive,
$20,000.'

Dollars were about four to the pound at that time. So
we drove out in a smart motor and were shown this
animal, quite a small two-year-old.

I was not very enamoured of it and said so. Bing said
it could perhaps win an early race. 'Could I not send it
straight away to Bernard van Cutsem for you?'

'Very well, why not? He's a mutual friend. We will
have it fifty-fifty between us.'

I told my people in England to pay the bill when
Frankie sent it to them from the Anglo-Irish agency.

A few days after I got back home, Bernard telephoned. 'Welcome home. Delighted to see you but

that little thing you sent, or Frankie sent, is so tiny that unless we win a race with it damn quick we won't win one at all.'

Worse was to come.

A letter soon appeared which read:

My dear, dear Porchey,

I cannot tell you how upset I am at having to write this letter to you but when I returned to England I found that all my financial affairs were in such a chaotic state that I would ask you – only ask you, naturally, for I would never go back on a pal – if you could take over the whole of this animal? It would be the greatest relief to me in my present circumstances. Yours, Frankie.

Being devoted to Frankie, Angela and all the children, I said I would, cursing under my breath that I had ever been to Beverly Hills, let alone seen the animal.

Two months elapsed. Bernard said that it was as slow as Puss in Boots.

So that was that. I sent it to the Ascot sales and reckoned whatever I could get for it would be a bonus because it would never win anything and once sold I wouldn't have to pay for its keep any longer.

9
Happy Hunting in Days of Yore

I ONCE WENT on safari with three friends, Myrtle and 'Flash' Kellet and an American girl Patty Hoyt. Patty loved everything to do with wild life and photography and the four of us started off from Nairobi. We had a very happy time and, on our return to civilization, I gave each of the girls a gold cigarette case with a map of our safari engraved on it, studded with different precious stones to mark the various places where we had spent the night.

I engaged a White Hunter whose name happened to be 'Hunter' and in his book he devoted a whole chapter to my adventures. Whilst under his guidance, I shot two black-maned lions, which I now regret, for there is no satisfaction in shooting a lion with a double-barrelled rifle when it is only about one hundred and fifty yards away. I did shoot a leopard which was sitting up on his haunches about three hundred yards away. It was a fluke that I got him as it was in the gloaming and he was difficult to see. I had the skin in my sitting-room for many years. One of the most remarkable shots I brought off was when I fired at a ten-year-old cock ostrich who was about four hundred yards away. I aimed at his body and succeeded in cutting his neck in half!

One day Flash damaged his finger while repairing the fan belt of the car. Luckily, I had some local anaesthetic in my first aid kit which I used to freeze his finger. I then removed his nail with a scalpel and bandaged it up. On our return to Nairobi, he saw a doctor who was quite astonished that a layman, such as I, had been able to do such a good job. I am pleased to say that the nail grew again.

There was a very unpleasant incident one day when we stopped for lunch beneath the shade of a big banyan tree. Our boys put a tarpaulin on the ground and both girls flopped down, glad of a rest and longing for a drink. They leapt up with a start almost immediately and shouted that something was wriggling. To our amazement, we realized that the boys unknowingly had thrown the tarpaulin down on top of an enormous python. I ran and got my shotgun and when he reared up, I shot him through the head. He was skinned by the boys who were very excited and pleased as they like eating the flesh – I cannot imagine why – and the girls had shoes and handbags made from the skin.

People's ideas are very different nowadays and I am in complete agreement with those who think it is far more fun to photograph animals rather than shoot them.

I didn't return to Africa again for some years, not until after the war, when I stayed one winter at the Mamounia Hotel in Marrakech. At that time, Winston and Clemmie were also there as Winston had suffered a stroke and was recuperating.

He did a good deal of painting in the mornings and much of the rest of the day he spent dozing in the sunshine, watched by his faithful English detective who was never far from his side.

In the evenings, he sometimes dined upstairs in his suite, which was virtually the whole of the first floor of the hotel except for the two rooms which I occupied, and after dinner, we often played a mild game of poker which Winston thoroughly enjoyed.

On my last evening there, I gave a large party in the dining-room downstairs and put Winston between Jacqueline Descamps and Tina Onassis and he was in his best form.

At the end of dinner, Jacqueline produced a tiny little toy pistol, about an inch long, from her handbag which used a cap that went off with a loud bang. She asked Winston, in a whisper, if she might fire it underneath the table because she thought it would be fun to see the reaction of his English detective who was eating alone at a table not far from where my party was assembled. Winston entered into the spirit of the joke and said, 'Yes, of course, my dear, let it off now.'

I knew nothing about this plot and as we were at the port and brandy stage and everyone was being very convivial, a loud report was heard from under the table. The detective leapt to his feet with his automatic at the ready and stared round the room. Winston waved his hand to his guardian to signify that he was all right and no further action was necessary. Clemmie, who was next to me, took a poor view of this practical joke and asked me if it had been planned. I replied that I knew absolutely nothing about it, which was the truth, the whole truth and nothing but the truth.

A monster poker party assembled in Winston's room and the evening ended on a very happy note. I gave his detective a bottle of Bollinger to drink my health and begged his forgiveness.

On my last visit to Africa, I flew out to Rhodesia and, on arrival, I went to Merkil's Hotel in Salisbury. Alec Home had asked me to take a letter to Ian Smith and requested me to bring back any reply there might be from Mr Smith which I did in due course.

I met Mr Smith at Government House and found him fascinating. He had been a fighter pilot and he always sat so that one could only see the right side of his face as he had a big scar from a bullet wound on his left cheek. I was most impressed by his conversation as we walked in the serenity of the gardens of Government House. It was a pleasure to hear his views. He struck me as a great patriot with an overwhelming desire for his country's well-being. Rhodesia was going through a rough time as Britain had declared his government illegal. I would have liked to see more of him. I did go at a later date to a cocktail party in Government House where I met a great many of his friends but, to my mind, the premier was the outstanding figure.

Living in Rhodesia at that time was a very old friend of mine, Margot Lorne, whose maiden name was Margot Mills. She was first married to John Chesham and after his death she remarried.

At the time of which I am writing, Eric Stocks was staying with her, another very old friend of mine, and he and I played golf at the Country Club. I was introduced there to many prominent people and one of them was a most interesting man, Peter Van der Byl, a member of Smith's cabinet. He told me I must see the Zambezi Falls and he arranged that a senior police officer would meet me at the Rhodesian side of the bridge over the Zambezi.

I flew down in a small aircraft and when I met the police officer, he told me that Queen Elizabeth, the Queen Mother, had opened the bridge when it was ready for use. By this time, however, the Zambian government had closed their end of this splendid construction and there was a small strip on the bridge called No Man's Land which marked the end of the Rhodesian side and the commencement of the Zambian side. To make me feel thoroughly at ease, he then told me that machine guns were constantly trained on the bridge to deal with any intruders who might feel so bold as to advance beyond the demarcation line.

Subsequently, I went up-country and saw many farms with excellent cattle, splendid schools for the locals and good clinics. I saw everything I possibly could during my six weeks' visit. All the local people I came across appeared to be very happy and during my séjour I never heard of any terrorist activity. Now, sadly, acts of terrorism seem to be an almost daily occurrence.

I consider Rhodesia to be by far the most attractive of the many African states that I've seen and it is a tragedy that so much suffering has been brought to that fair and pleasant land.

10
Love and Laughter in America

I HAVE VISITED the United States many times over the years. I remember vividly the first time I went there for I sailed in a ship called the *Aquitania* which was not very comfortable and we arrived in New York after eight rough days at sea.

We had to be preceded by an ice-breaker before we could tie up at our berth on the pier. New York was bitterly cold and the majority of the people living there walked about the streets wearing earflaps and astrakhan hats.

It may interest readers to know that as a result of the Gulf Stream moving so many miles to the south in recent years, the climate in New York is now very mild compared to what it was fifty years ago. Nowadays I am often able to walk about the city during the winter months without wearing an overcoat.

America was very different from anything I had ever known. To start with the people were very hospitable and I was a guest of dear old Ambrose Clark. I got to know many of his friends, the women being very friendly and charming to talk to and dance with but, if they were 'genuine' Americans, they were very straight-laced. They did not respond as women did in

Europe so I was hesitant about making a pass at them because I thought it likely that I'd have my face slapped!

On another occasion when Valentine Castlerosse and I were in California together, Valentine suggested that we should go out to St Simeon and visit William Randolph Hearst who was a press baron and thought himself a very important man in the States. His place was designed, I think, as a copy of an old English castle and he had suits of armour of all kinds there. When we were shown into the great man's presence, he glowered at me and said, 'Tell me, my boy, are you anti-American like I am anti-English?'

I replied that I had such happy times in America that I was certainly not anti-American.

'Well,' he said, 'I'm definitely anti-English!'

As he was a much older man than I, I decided to call it a day and asked if I might be shown round his property with all its British trappings!

In the summer of 1938, I was travelling to America on the *Queen Mary*. My friends Noel Coward and Randolph Churchill were on board and for some reason or other, they did not like each other.

Noel told me that he had just delivered a note to Randolph's cabin, reading as follows:

Dear Randolph,

If you are free, I hope you will come to the first night of my new show which opens next week. I enclose a brace of tickets so that you may bring a friend, if you have one.

Randolph, who was always a cheeky monkey, wrote back as follows:

Dear Noel,

Unfortunately I am engaged on the opening night of your show. Nevertheless, I shall be delighted to come on another night, if you have one!

Some of my lady readers may use Elizabeth Arden cosmetics and, if so, they may be interested to know what Mrs Graham, the founder of this company, was really like.

Having made a vast fortune from her business, she went into racing in a big way. On one occasion, when I was attending the yearling sales in Kentucky, she asked me to look at some of the choicest lots and give her my opinion about them. I duly inspected the yearlings and gave her my advice.

The sales are always held at night and everybody sits in their allotted seats, the men usually wearing dinner jackets, and the bidding comes fast and furious from all over the ring. It is really quite exciting for anyone who has not seen how these auctions are conducted in the United States.

After this particular sale, I had made a booking for myself and my valet to return to New York by air. However, Mrs Graham's manager came to me and said, 'Mrs Graham would like you to accompany her to New York in her private plane.'

I replied that my valet would have to come with me and he assured me that there was plenty of room and so I accepted the kind offer and cancelled my booking.

You will find it almost unbelievable, but about fifteen minutes before we were due to land, this man leaned over my seat and said, 'Lord Carnarvon, I have to ask you for $600 for your two seats.'

I told him I was astounded that he should make such a suggestion and that I had not the slightest intention of paying Mrs Graham anything, as I had been invited to fly back as her guest!

With regard to her racing interests, this woman had endless trainers which is one of the greatest mistakes any owner can make. In her crazy fashion, she always insisted that her creams and lotions should be used if any of her horses suffered an injury.

She had a brilliant brain for business but knew nothing about horse racing and many of the people concerned with her affairs told me she was quite impossible to deal with.

I frequently stayed with Consuelo and Jacques Balsan in their beautiful house on Hypolluxa Island which is very close to Palm Beach, Florida, for Bert Marlborough was Consuelo's eldest son by her first marriage.

I well remember one particular occasion when they gave a luncheon party to which a South American gentleman, who was an ambassador in Washington, came accompanied by his lovely wife and the first secretary at his embassy.

I was sitting close to Jacques who had placed the

South American beauty on his right hand, ostensibly as she did not speak much English. The first secretary was put on her other side. Dear Jacques, running true to form, attempted to play 'footsie' with the lovely lady but she had carefully tucked her feet well under her chair and in the process he missed her and kept pressing the foot of the first secretary.

The first secretary did not react but when luncheon was over, he went up to Consuelo and said, *'Excusez-moi, madame, mais est ce que ce monsieur là est légèrement pédéraste?'*

Consuelo drew herself up to her full height and replied, *'Sûrement pas. Mon mari malheureusement est toujours coureur.'*

This event created quite a storm in a teacup, much to the amusement of all who were present and particularly to Consuelo's son who considered it one of the most hilarious happenings he had ever witnessed.

On another visit to America, Hugh Sefton and I were staying in Palm Beach and we were invited to dinner by Laddie Sandford and his charming wife, Mary. It was the custom in Palm Beach in those days to have large dinner parties and there were about forty guests.

After the first course had been served, which was a soup called clam chowder, there was a long pause. Four servants came in, each carrying a large platter of meat. The moment they entered the room a most horrible smell permeated the atmosphere.

When the waiter got near to Hugh, who was sitting on Mary's right, he said to her, 'Good God, Mary, what the devil is this awful stuff? It stinks to high heaven!'

'It's moose. Laddie shot it last year and we put it in the deep freeze to save it for a special occasion.'

The smell was so pungent that all the windows had to be flung wide open. After a long delay, some cold ham was served to the hungry guests, followed by the usual vanilla ice-cream with fresh strawberries, which I have found to be tasteless when grown in Florida. Not a patch on those from Highclere.

In the course of my peregrinations abroad, I have encountered a great many distinguished Americans and become good friends with a number of them.

I had a great regard for General Eisenhower whom I met when he was commanding the American Forces during the Second World War, and which lasted all through the years of his presidency until his death. He was a remarkably fine man and his honesty and breadth of vision, coupled with immense tact, endeared him to many. It was a rare experience, and a very refreshing one, to hear in private from Ike what he thought about Monty and, in inverse ratio, I learned from old Monty his views on the Supreme Commander of the Allied Armies!

Lewis Douglas, who was American Ambassador at the Court of St James, was a very good-looking man and had a charming disposition. A good sportsman, he loved fly fishing and it was a tragedy when, casting for a wily trout, he caught the fishhook in his eye and, as a result, lost the sight from that eye. I cannot think of any better representative, during my lifetime, who has graced the United States Embassy.

Joseph Kennedy was a very different character. I first met him when I was staying in Palm Beach, Florida, in 1928. At that time, he had made a large fortune speculating in stocks and shares. One day, when walking with him in his garden, he made a proposition to me which I thought, to say the least, a very cheeky one. He suggested that I should have a small office in London and that he would call me up from time to time, the idea being that I was to tell my numerous friends and acquaintances to buy a certain security which he hoped would go up and Joe would then sell his holding in that company and would cut me in for a percentage each time a deal was satisfactorily concluded.

I was horrified that he should imagine that I would be a party to anything of the sort and I told him so without mincing my words! He did not seem to think that he had suggested anything untoward and that was the end of the matter – stillborn in every respect.

It is the fashion nowadays to say *'de mortuis nil nisi bonum'* but I personally subscribe to the view that it is more correct to say 'the evil that men do lives after them'. Although Kennedy was made Ambassador to Great Britain in 1938, I never had any truck with him then or later.

An American who impressed me was Bernard Baruch, a very canny politician. He was a bosom friend of Winston Churchill's and I first met him at his home in South Carolina.

Baruch was born in 1870 and died in 1965. I shall always remember him as a true patriot in an era when

that commodity was still fashionable. He was however
a Jew and told me once, quite without bitterness, that
he considered he might have been president had he not
been Jewish. He was actually attacked very fiercely by
old Henry Ford in the 1920s, which was rather sad,
because he had done so much to help various presidents
at critical times in the history of the United States. He
had a curious affection for anything to do with farming. I found this very strange as the investment of
money and speculation of many kinds was really his
métier.

Walter Annenberg was one of the more recent
ambassadors who gave great pleasure to many. He
spent much of his vast fortune refurbishing Winfield
House in Regent's Park and the glorious parties that he
gave were the highlights of the social scene in the
metropolis.

When I was in Washington, for the opening of the
Tutankhamun Exhibition in 1976, I was very anxious
to have a look at the State Rooms in the White House. I
knew the public were admitted each day at 9 am and I
asked President Ford's secretary if I might come at
8 am, with my butler, Robert Taylor, and Miss Vicky
Wayne, who was appointed by Exxon to see that I met
all my commitments, such as radio and TV interviews,
and this request was granted.

We walked to the White House which was just a few
minutes from The Hay-Adams Hotel and I carried a
copy of my book *No Regrets* which I had autographed
and intended presenting to President Ford who was

then in Palm Springs. At the entrance, the guard on duty said, 'Mr *Carnavon*, we know you are due here this morning but I must have some identification. Have you got your passport with you?'

I told him I had left my passport in the hotel, and then I was struck by a sudden brainwave. On the back of my book there is a fairly good photograph of me and when I showed him this, he was entirely satisfied.

In the White House, I was met by a charming girl called Barbara who worked there. Having signed the Visitors' Book, I gave her the copy of *No Regrets* to await the president's return. I later received a charming letter from him saying how much he had enjoyed it.

I always carry a walking stick with me which has a rubber tip on the end. I use it to rest on, as my legs get very tired when I have to stand for any length of time. Barbara pointed out that 'canes' as they are called in the States, are not allowed in the State Rooms. I told her that I really could not manage to go round without my stick to rest on. She offered to supply me with an invalid chair. I firmly declined and as the stick has paid visits to Buckingham Palace without doing the slightest damage I felt that it might be allowed the same courtesy in the White House. Eventually agreement was reached and she said she would broadcast to the guards in each of the rooms telling them that I had a special dispensation and was allowed to keep my stick.

We proceeded through the rooms very happily until we arrived in the State Dining-Room where all the gold plate is locked in show-cases. I spotted a lovely photograph of the Queen and the Duke of Edinburgh and as I walked towards it, pointing with my stick, I said to Vicky, 'This is one of the best photographs I have ever seen of the Queen.'

At that moment a guard burst in through a door left slightly ajar, with his revolver pointing at my navel!

'What's that?' he roared, and I replied that it was my shooting stick.

'Drop it, drop it!' he shouted, which I did, pronto! After all, there are no medals for getting shot in the White House.

'Put your hands up,' he continued, so I obeyed his orders immediately and he approached rather gingerly with his gun still pointing at my tummy.

'How come you've got that shooting stick?'

I explained that Barbara had broadcast before I began my tour and that my stick was completely harmless and used by me only for resting my aged body. He put his gun away, shook hands with me and said, 'I'm mighty sorry about this. I must have been in the "john" when Miss Barbara broadcast. I do apologize, sir.'

We became buddies after this and he said that he would like a copy of *No Regrets* to remind him of a momentous visit by the only earl he had ever met. I sent him my book as soon as I could.

In February 1978, I revisited Palm Beach. I was last there about fifteen years ago. On this occasion, I had the joy of dining at Amado, a lovely home where I had stayed so often in the past with Charles A. Munn, known to all and sundry as Mr Palm Beach. A lifelong friend of mine, he is a most remarkable man, a nonagenarian and extremely good looking. About twenty years ago he married his second wife whose maiden name was Dorothy Spreckles, affectionately known as 'Sugar' Spreckles, as her family fortune was derived from sugar cane.

Dorothy has a passion for playing bridge, which she indulges by taking part in many tournaments and I believe she is often successful, which is not surprising, as she has always been a skilful player with a natural flair for the game. Her husband does not much care for cards but enjoys showing any good films he can find at his lovely house, usually preceded by a large dinner party.

At one of these parties I heard the following tales which I trust will make my readers chuckle as indeed I did.

When the new Pope came to his high office, he said to his Cardinal Secretary of State, 'Tell me, my friend, I have been wondering what is in that old box. It looks as if it has been here for thousands of years. Do you have a key?'

'Yes, Your Holiness,' he replied. 'I shall fetch it immediately.'

When he returned with the key, the Pope unlocked the box. He looked inside, gave a grunt, shut up the box and kept the key.

The cardinal could contain his curiosity no longer.

'Your Holiness, forgive my impertinence but I am very curious to know what you saw in the box.'

The Pope replied, 'A bill for the Last Supper.'

A commercial traveller flew from New York to Houston, Texas, to sell his wares. He spied a cosy-looking saloon bar, entered and ordered himself a cold beer.

He heard some customers discussing local politics and wanting to appear friendly, he said to them, 'Say folks, I think Carter is a horse's ass!'

Two huge Texans immediately picked him up bodily and dumped him in the street outside. After a moment or two, he got up, dusted himself down and went back to pay for his drink.

Approaching the bar, he said, 'Gee folks, I'm real sorry about what I said. I had no idea this was Carter country.'

A shout went up.

'It ain't Carter country, buddy, it's horse country!'

11
Precious Pals

WHEN I WAS SEVENTEEN, I became friends with one of the most attractive men I have ever met, Fred Cripps, son of the first Lord Parmoor. He had worked before the war for Bolton Brothers in Russia. Shortly after the declaration of war in 1914, he returned to fight for his King and country.

He was Colonel of the Bucks Hussars, a Yeomanry regiment, and among the officers of the regiment were Tony and Evelyn de Rothschild. Because of the Jewish element, there was a soubriquet which amused the troops: 'No Advance Without Security.' They were a splendid lot of chaps and Fred, one of the bravest, earned a DSO and Bar, which he richly deserved.

I well remember him having one of his many love affairs with a charming American actress called Teddy Gerrard. I used to tuck them up in those days in his flat, 17 Sackville Street, and it amused me to see that Teddy had decorated the bedroom with mauve wallpaper, mauve curtains, mauve sheets and pillows on which rested a lilac nightie and on the bedside table, a huge box of chocolate creams with violets on every one. Fred and she made a splendid couple and I had great fun with them.

Teddy used to sing this song on the stage:

Everybody calls me Teddy,
T.E. Double D.Y.
Yankees waiting, all expectating
With the R.S.V.P. Eye.
All day long my telephone
Keeps ringing me hard,
Are you there?
Little Teddy bear,
Naughty, naughty one Gerrard!

Fred passed away recently at the ripe old age of ninety-two. I miss him greatly as he was a true friend, one of a fast diminishing band.

Another of the pals was Harry Rosebery, whom I often think about. I also knew his father but I never cared much for him. He struck me as being a mean little man, an ex-Liberal prime minister who had won the Derby no less than three times. Most people count themselves lucky to win the Derby once.

Dick Dawson trained a filly of his who was well handicapped in the Cambridgeshire and he wrote to Harry telling him that his father's filly had a very good chance of winning. Harry immediately put a couple of hundred quid on the filly at 33/1. (Ante-post betting in those days was quite different from now and book-makers of the calibre of Goll of Liverpool and others would lay you bets of that sort without batting an eyelid. Nowadays, if you want to strike a wager on a race such as the Cambridgeshire, you are limited by many of the advertising bookmakers to only winning a monkey, which is racing slang for £500, at the quoted odds.)

On learning that his son had backed her without telling him anything about it, the old man promptly scratched her.

Harry was born at Mentmore and in my opinion, its recent sale with all the contents was a sad day for England. I shall never know why the government did not take over the whole caboodle. Had they done so, they would have made an excellent investment as well as preserving a priceless national heritage.

Harry's father was invited one day to lunch with the Fishmongers, a livery company in London, and every kind of trouble had been taken to make this a notable occasion. When he rose to respond to the toast, he started by saying, 'I have a serious complaint to make.'

Everyone wondered what on earth had gone wrong and you could have heard a pin drop. After a pause, he said, 'I've eaten too much!'

That brought the house down and everything was *couleur de rose*.

Nevertheless, in my book, he remains a mean old devil who was horrible to Harry.

In those days parents and children often seemed to be at odds, It was not always easy for outsiders to understand what the battles were about: it might be a long-standing family feud, a personal private vendetta or, as in the case of Emerald and Nancy Cunard, their respective lovers.

Emerald Cunard was a vivacious little creature who never stopped talking. One of the best-known hostesses of that era, she held regular luncheon parties at her London house, which I often attended. There I would meet famous political figures of the time who were frequently invited.

Emerald's lover was the famous conductor, Sir Thomas Beecham, who was a curious creature. I did not particularly care for him but a great many people thought he was very good value and, no doubt, they were quite correct in their judgement. If there were no differences of opinion, there would be no fancy waist-coats.

I preferred Emerald's daughter Nancy, who was a very good-looking girl. She was of the same vintage as Diana Manners of whom Nancy was inordinately jeal-ous. She had every reason to be, as Diana was one of the most beautiful girls imaginable and had played the part of the nun in a wonderful play called *The Miracle*, in which my second wife Tilly Losch had had a small part. Max Reinhardt who directed the play, was fond of both of them. I greatly enjoyed the company of Diana, who married Alfred Duff Cooper. He amused us all by going red with rage, like a small turkey cock, whenever his political opinions were gainsaid. Still he was always a lively member of Emerald's luncheon parties.

Nancy seldom turned up at her mother's house for she preferred to lead a more exotic life of her own. Her love life appeared to be of a thoroughly promiscuous nature and rumour had it that it would not have been impossible for a black piccaninny to appear on the scene.

London life in those halcyon days was full of spice.
Each decided to forget the horrors of war in his or her
own way, but most chose to lose themselves in activity, in parties, entertainments, good talk, gossip and
amusement. It was not a happy time for everyone, far
from it, many were miserable under the surface, others
were broke and not a few found the strain too great,
but it was certainly lively and gregarious. It was a time
for friends and for companionship. One of those who
seemed to be enjoying himself at the time was the then
Prince of Wales. He and I frequently went to the theatre
together, for a box at the Windmill Theatre was per-
manently at his disposal, and from time to time he
would ring me up suggesting that I might like to
accompany him that evening as he and 'Fruity' Met-
calfe were going to the theatre and hoped to take
Dorothy Campbell and 'Bubbles' Ryan and perhaps
Sylvia Ashley to the Embassy Club for dinner afterwards.

Once Nancy Ryan became very distressed because
HRH had gone backstage earlier than usual and she had
bumped into him. (She always said she knocked him
over, but I don't agree.) She was in a great taradiddle
over this silly little incident but the Prince never gave it
a thought.

Darling Nancy became 'Bubbles' Holmes and she
and her husband winter annually in their charming
house in Nassau. At the time of writing, I am delighted
to say she is in great form, still playing golf almost as
well as ever and remains one of my dearest friends.
Sylvia Ashley is hale and hearty and so is Dorothy
Campbell, one of the most beautiful girls I've ever
known.

We were all great pals and spent many happy evenings at the Embassy where champagne flowed and
Luigi, the head waiter, always provided cold quails in
aspic, for which he knew HRH had a great liking.

The King used to ask me to some of the state balls at
Buckingham Palace when exquisite ladies in magnifi-
cent dresses thronged the rooms. When Prince George,
Duke of Kent, became engaged to Princess Marina, a
particularly fine ball was given in their honour. The
Princess was outstandingly lovely and as Prince
George was a very good-looking man, they made a
striking couple.

Whilst Prince George was passing through the room
with his fiancée, he was continually stopping to intro-
duce her to his many friends who were lined up on
both sides.

After he had introduced me to the Princess and we
had had a short chat, they moved on, and the Prince of
Wales, who was following some way behind, did me
the honour of stopping for a few moments. I thought
he looked somewhat disconsolate at the adulation they
were receiving and I formed the impression that he was
feeling rather lonely.

I was fond of dancing and it was considered the right
thing to do to dance the first dance of the evening with
one's wife, if one had a wife. This custom, I fear, never
appealed to me as I felt that I spent a great deal of time
with my wife and, consequently, preferred to dis-
regard it.

Supper was a somewhat formal affair – the band
stopped playing and the dining-rooms were opened.
The tables groaned with masses of delicious cold
foods, such as very fat quails in aspic, these having been

imported live from Egypt and kept in a dark cellar at Bailey's, the famous poulterers. Four or five times a day the electric lights were turned on and the silly quails thought it was morning and started to feed each time this was done, thereby fattening themselves up and speeding the day of their demise.

The supper tables were all of different proportions, some capable of seating eight, some twelve and some twenty-four. I believe that even at Buckingham Palace, which was full of footmen in livery, the staff were helped by many of their friends who worked at the big houses in London and whose employers had been invited to the ball.

State balls were much more to my liking than coronations when one had to dress up in such hot and heavy finery and stand about for interminable hours. I have attended three and the first was certainly the most arduous, when I was a trainbearer to George v in 1911. Of the eight pages, all except Bunny Romilly and I have gone the way of all flesh. Later I was present at the coronation of both King George vi and our present Queen, at both of which I wore the robes which had originally belonged to my father.

When I took my seat in the abbey on the latter occasion, I found an old friend, Field-Marshal Lord Montgomery, tapping me on the shoulder and saying, 'How is it that you, a Belted Earl, should have a good position where you can see all that is going on when I, a Field-Marshal recently made a Viscount, am so badly placed that I am unable to see anything?'

'My dear Field-Marshal', said I, 'please take my place. I have seen several coronations and I am only too delighted for you to sit in my seat.'

'Many thanks', said Monty, 'but I would not dream of exchanging places for a very good reason. I am much nearer to the WC than you are. When you are my age, you will find that very important.'

When the Queen of Tonga arrived to take her seat in the abbey – she must have been about seven feet tall and was indubitably the biggest woman I have ever seen – she was accompanied by a tiny little man.

'Look at that enormous woman and her little escort,' said an English peer, 'who can he be?'

'He's her lunch!' was the reply.

On so many convivial occasions when spirits were high and life was at its most enjoyable, a frequent companion would be my old school friend Bert Marlborough. We would meet at many of the events I have just been describing and we would also often spend the weekend in each other's company. I was playing bridge with him at Blenheim one day when a footman appeared to announce that there was a personal call for his grace from Athens.

Bert said he thought it would probably be Stavros Niarchos inviting him to shoot at Spetsapoulos. Bert and I had shot there on two previous occasions. Thousands of pheasants were reared, as well as partridges, on this tiny island which was not more than six miles long and flat as a pancake. I remember, with disgust, those low pheasants which were of no interest to anyone and the partridges, even more pathetic, were driven towards the sea which, of course, they could not face, with the result that most of them could have been caught in a butterfly net. Except for the midday bathe, followed by an excellent lunch and a delightful dinner in the balmy Aegean air, I could find nothing to enthuse about and had no desire to return.

Bert felt exactly as I did so he told his footman to say he was out and returned to the bridge table to find I had won him the rubber. His only comment was, 'If you had bid differently, we could probably have arrived at a slam.'

It was frequently said about him that whoever his partner might be, he was always the worst player at the Portland Club! I have no delusions about my skill at the game, nevertheless I refused to be bullied by my old chum and we got on splendidly on the green baize although somewhat less well on his beautiful croquet lawn.

He took croquet very seriously, although playing for small sums, usually a bob a hoop, and cursed me loudly if I failed to execute a 'stop shot' and left my own ball in a position that he did not like. On balance we usually won which was the main consideration from his point of view.

A game I greatly enjoyed playing was polo which I first learnt in India where I played for my regiment and took part in several tournaments, our team having the luck to win the Ezra Cup in Calcutta and the Dhar tournament in Mhow. We also triumphed in Bombay watched by the governor. But the finest match of all was when the 7th Hussars competed against the 11th Hussars at Meerut in the final of the Inter-Regimental in front of the viceroy, Lord Reading.

It was a magnificent occasion but during the match my stick became entangled in the bridle of John

Coombe's pony and pulled it clean off. The referee blew his whistle and the chukka was halted whilst the bridle was replaced. It was an extraordinary thing to happen but it certainly gave us a breathing space. As we were all square at the end of six chukkas, the goal-posts were widened and my mare, Polly, whom I had bought from Dolly Melville, then Colonel of the 17th Lancers, was closely pursued by one of the players in the opposing team who was about to hook my stick had I raised it in the normal fashion. I did the next best thing. With a stiff forearm I pushed the ball which, happily, hit the basket of the goal-post and trickled over the line. The linesman raised his flag denoting that we had scored a goal and won the tournament. The viceroy then presented us with the cup and my beloved wife Catherine, was probably the most excited of our many supporters.

On one of the few occasions that I ever played polo in England I played for the House of Lords against the House of Commons in a game at Roehampton. The Commons' team won, which was not surprising as they had better players, better ponies and were vigorously captained by Winston Churchill, who had little hesitation in riding you off if he thought he could hit the ball better as a result of his efforts. It was all good fun and I was devoted to him, spending a good deal of time in his company.

As I never attained anything better than a four-goal handicap, I was particularly pleased to be invited to play polo in Hollywood with Louis B. Mayer's team. He was President of 20th Century Fox at the time and we had many amusing games in which we were ably assisted by Ian Balding's father who was appointed by

Louis to be team manager. Everything was for free and I was entertained handsomely.

Victor McLaghlen, who played the lead in *The Four Feathers* had been a sergeant under my command during the First World War. After the end of hostilities, he returned to Hollywood and resumed his film career. I was so pleased to meet him again and I have a charming photograph of him with Claudette Colbert. He introduced me to many of the famous film stars of that era. Carole Lombard, for instance, was married at that time to Clark Gable with whom I used to play golf when not required for any other activity. I found them to be an extremely nice couple. I think, in those days, people in the film industry tended to remain married longer than they seem to do at the present time.

Katharine Hepburn, 'married' to the great Spencer Tracy, was also very kind to me. One day, I was returning from America by air and Tracy was on the plane. Half-way across the Atlantic, the pilot announced that one of the engines had failed and that he would have to return to New York flying at about two thousand feet in order to conserve the petrol. Spencer drank a great deal of booze on the return journey and when we eventually arrived safely at the airport about 2 am I shall never forget him saying to me, 'Are all the God-damned British like you? I was so scared that I got well and truly stoned and you never blinked an eyelid! Will you help me drink a bottle of champagne before we take off again?'

Perhaps the actress who surprised me most was Marilyn Monroe. I had always thought of her as she was depicted in the innumerable photographs which soldiers, sailors and airmen had pinned up in barracks and offices all over the world in the 1950s. In these pin-ups, her face shone forth like a beacon to gladden the heart of every fighting man; all revealed her as a very delectable dish. In real life she seemed so very different to the glamorous creature which I had conjured up in my imagination. Nor did she seem to have much of a sense of humour which, to me, is very important. All my illusions were shattered when I met her.

Humphrey Bogart was another friend, a wonderful man and a really great actor. Always fun to be with, he was very attractive to women. He certainly had charisma for his rugged visage did not entitle him to be called an Adonis!

When I took out one of the Hollywood beauties, my favourite 'muy simpatica' companion was that most delightful lady Merle Oberon. She had everything a man could desire, beautiful looks and considerable intelligence. All the men who knew her felt they could never be happier than in her arms. They got no further.

At one time this affectionate creature had been in love with my dear friend Prince Aly Khan, father of Karim, who has now become the present Aga Khan. It was a tremendous shock to her when Aly departed for pastures new. I tried to help her over this depressing period of her life. She was a good companion even in distress and we used to have many dinners and luncheons together whilst she talked and talked about her love for Aly. We would go to Romanov's, The Brown Derby or to Chasens which were all places much favoured by the film industry. However two tiresome ladies were generally present, Louella Parsons and Hedda Hopper. They were both elderly dames when I knew them and I do not think either of them liked the other. They were bad news from my point of view because no matter who I took out, there were usually snide comments in their columns the following day to the effect that the good-looking young English Lord had found yet another new girlfriend!

I thought Mike Romanoff was one of the biggest phoneys that ever existed. He informed me one day that he was a frequent visitor to Chatsworth and Blenheim but when I tested him on his knowledge of them he was completely nonplussed. He was a small ugly man who I believe had done 'time' in America. He styled himself 'Prince' Mike Romanoff, pretending he was related to the Tsar of All the Russias and his family. You can fool some of the people some of the time but you cannot fool all the people all of the time!

Whilst in Hollywood, I got to know some of the film directors very well because they often invited me to go on the set and watch them working.

I particularly liked John Huston, a great tall, craggy chap, who loved hunting and became a master of foxhounds in Ireland. He once offered me a part in a film he was producing. Unfortunately, I was unable to accept because I had too many other things to do at home at the time. On another occasion, he asked me to be technical director of a film which was to be made of the Battle of Omdurman and I was to advise on military details concerning the charge of the 21st Lancers. In the end, as far as I know, the film was never made.

Another very good director, Edmund Goulding, was a charming fellow. He worked for old Sam Goldwyn at MGM and although he was a very shy man, he was one hell of a director on the set. One of his great successes was *Dawn Patrol* in which Errol Flynn starred. Another was *Grand Hotel* with Joan Crawford and Greta Garbo in the leading parts.

On one occasion, Eddy Goulding told Irving Thalberg, the great producer, that he had a marvellous idea for a film and suggested that Jean Harlow and Clark Gable should be the stars. Thalberg agreed and everything was settled, including the money. When the time came for Thalberg to start work on it, Eddy had completely forgotten all about it. In the end, he got hold of another story which Thalberg accepted happily, being completely unaware that it was not the original one previously proposed by Eddy.

I have been told that at Eddy Goulding's funeral, people thought he had chosen the funniest collection of pall-bearers. They tried to lug the huge coffin up the mountainside and when they laid it down to have a rest because it was so heavy, the coffin slipped, careering madly down an incline towards where the grave was sited. Fortunately, it hit a headstone, which pulled it up. So ended an interment which must be unique even in that extraordinary atmosphere of Hollywood in those bygone days.

Now that I have become an author in my old age, I frequently reflect on the many writers I have known.

Somerset Maugham ranks as a prince of his profession but I found him unattractive. He seemed to have some stomach trouble as he kept taking tablets which he pulled out of his waistcoat pocket at frequent intervals. His wife, Syrie, was a totally different type, warm-hearted and cosy, with a chest on which the proverbial tea-tray could well have found a safe resting place!

Perhaps Ian Fleming gave me more pleasure than any other writer I knew – all his books were such fun and I never had a dull moment when I was with him. I played golf with him frequently in many parts of the world and had endless parties when staying with him in Jamaica where he loved to play cards. Bridge for choice, if he could arrange a nice rubber.

Noel Coward was a fairly near neighbour in Montego Bay and I saw a lot of him in those days – another charming pal whom I miss. He was the only man I have ever known who always called me 'Porchey Dolling' a form of address which stamped him as having slight homosexual tendencies. However, he never caused me, or any of my friends, the least embarrassment by his affectionate way of speaking and I miss this warm-hearted genius very much.

Leonora Corbett, an English actress, starred in Noel Coward's play *Blithe Spirit* when he first produced it.

She was the *chère amie* of a rich Dutchman àt whose castle in Holland I stayed on several occasions.

I thought Leonora had more brains than good looks but she was a talented actress and I found her to be a vivacious companion.

The Second World War put a stop to travel and entertaining but I still managed to see old friends, in particular Winston Churchill. In the early days of the war I was lunching with him at Chequers when he told me a very interesting little tale.

A man, dressed in civilian clothes and carrying a valise, arrived at Waverley Station in Edinburgh. He had a ticket to London and asked a porter to show him the way to the 'sleeping wagon'. That, of course, is not an expression which any Britisher would use. He would normally ask to be shown to the sleeper.

This intelligent porter associated 'sleeping wagon' with the German *schlafswagen* and having shown the man to the sleeping car, he immediately contacted the military police and told them of his suspicions. A police officer promptly boarded the train and asked to see the man's identity card. This was not quite as it should have been and the man was removed from the train for further investigation.

He was subsequently taken to the Tower of London where he was tried by court martial. At his trial, he confessed that he had landed from a German submarine and had been instructed to proceed to an address in London where he was to set up a radio transmitter.

As he had been caught and had not had time to do any harm to our war effort I asked Winston, who had told me this story, if the poor fellow would be shot.

'Certainly not!' he replied. 'I hope to get him down here to have a long talk with him. It will be most interesting for me to have a full account of his activities.'

He was imprisoned for the duration of the war but was, in due course, repatriated.

Winston also told me how much he admired my friend Bud Flanagan. 'Your pal has done more for us than most of my blooming generals,' he said. Bud Flanagan had been offered an enormous contract in America at this time, but he had refused to leave England: he felt that he could do more to help win the war by remaining here. 'If I go up to London from Brighton every morning and sing "Underneath the Arches" after a blitz, it revives morale and that helps those brave bombed folk to carry on. I *hate* those damned Nazis and will do everything I can to see they lose.' He was a great patriot and the much-loved Jewish star of the Crazy Gang, of whom the only survivor is dear old Chesney Allan. How I admired these great comedians.

Another friend I made during the war was General Patton who brought me all sorts of goodies from the PX. The most useful items he brought were golf balls – the dried onions and potato crisps I passed on to people who needed them. Happily, with my garden, I was more or less self-sufficient.

Just before the invasion of Normandy, I invited him and his ADC to lunch. It was a beautiful summer day and we were a party of about eight. During lunch, my

butler asked Patton's ADC if he would take red or white
wine, to which the boy replied, 'I'd like a glass of milk,
please.'

At this, his general threw him an appallingly dirty
look and said, 'My dear Tim, didn't you get enough of
that stuff at your mother's breast?'

The lad went the colour of beetroot and I felt very
sorry for him.

After lunch the general suggested that we should
take a walk together on the lawn and, whilst alone, he
said, 'Colonel, when we go into Normandy, I have one
plan and one plan only. I am not going to listen to Ike
or Monty because I am determined to get to Berlin
before those God-damned Russians. If they get there
before we do, the whole war will have been in vain
because those bloody Bolsheviks will think they've
done it alone and all our efforts will have been
nullified.'

I wept when I heard the sad news of his death.

12
High Pheasants

I WAS NEVER taught to shoot by anybody. I think it came more or less naturally to me. My father was one of the best shots in England for many years, I was given a single-barrelled 410 gun to start with and I tried to shoot rabbits, which were numerous, with my father's head keeper, a charming old boy called Henry Maber. When I was around fourteen, I graduated to a single-barrelled sixteen bore non-ejector gun, the theory being that with young people, it was better to make them remove the cartridges themselves.

One day, Lord de Grey, later to become Marquis of Ripon, was staying here. He was one of the best shots in England, extremely jealous and a thoroughly selfish and spoilt old man. My father used to shoot grouse with him at Ripon and the whole moor was always driven so that de Grey would get the shooting. On this occasion, old de Grey missed a cock pheasant – which was most unusual – and I happened to 'wipe his eye'. I made a big mistake because for the rest of the day anything that looked as if it might be coming my way was executed by him.

In 1922, when I was soldiering at York, I was invited to shoot by a curious character called The Hon. Charles

Hanbury, Lord Bateman's brother, who had a shoot near Diss in Norfolk. I took a nice young soldier to load for me. The sun blazed down on this lovely September day and having been introduced to the other guns, I went to my butt. I waited for quite some time, dozing happily in the sunshine, when I spotted my host hurrying towards me.

'My dear Porchey,' he said, 'have you any money on you?' When I told him I had about thirty pounds, he asked if I would give him the lot as he needed it to pay the beaters or they would not proceed. Apparently he had not paid them for the last two shoots and they had gone on strike. He went round collecting money from all the guns and assured us we would be repaid at luncheon. After this interminable delay, we had a very enjoyable morning with quite a lot of partridges in the bag.

At lunchtime I expected to be repaid but nothing was forthcoming, so I was left in the unenviable position of having no money with which to tip the head keeper. I told him I had no cash on me and sent him a cheque as soon as I got back to barracks.

It is interesting to reflect that in those days at many shooting parties, especially on grouse moors and partridge shooting, the guns were given a packet of sandwiches, a slice of cake, an apple and a bottle of beer and they considered themselves lucky if they got a cold drink at the end of the day while the bag was being counted by the keepers.

Nowadays, with the advent of jeeps and Land Rovers, all sorts of refreshments are brought out, hot soup which everyone enjoys, lots of sloe gin, home-made cherry brandy and an exotic drink called Southern Comfort which keeps everyone content until they get back for lunch.

I think people had more consideration for their employees in the old days and never shot if the weather was inclement. Nowadays, hosts do not want to disappoint their guests and most of them wish to get their game killed because pheasants sell well in the early part of the season.

Another great difference is that in these difficult days there are as many as ten guns pheasant shooting. When I was young, there were seldom more than four or five.

I am lucky enough to have several grandsons who love shooting. Harry Herbert, Porchester's younger boy, has the making of a first-rate shot and his elder son, Geordie, is also a good shot. I am sure that when they have had more practise, they will be as good as their father. My daughter Penelope's son, David, is also mad keen on shooting but as he is a hard-working banker, he gets few opportunities to display his skill.

I don't want my readers to think that I am emulating Muhammed Ali because I would deplore it if they did. However, I can claim to be a knowledgeable person where rearing of game and the showing of birds is concerned in order to give the people who are going to shoot them real pleasure.

The actual production of eggs for hatching has not altered since I was a boy: large aviaries are still constructed of timber and wire netting in convenient sheltered spots and keepers still proceed to catch young pheasants, starting in February, and place them in the aviaries at a ration of eight hens to one cock. The birds are then fed very well and start to lay in early April. But rearing pheasants has undergone many changes over the past decades for it is now a very expensive business using electric incubators, whereas it used to involve only broody hens. Today the keepers set the eggs for three weeks in large incubators which can take many thousands of eggs. Then the eggs are transferred to a special still air incubator where after three days, with a bit of luck, they will begin to hatch. Luck plays an essential part and with good management added, it is now possible to achieve an average of sixty-five per cent live chicks to eggs set.

The tiny chicks are then put under infra-red lamps in brooder houses for up to six weeks and fed on a special crumbly mixture of vitamins and proteins which is obtained from an animal feed firm. After six weeks in the brooder house, the poults, as they are now called, are transferred into the release pens which are in various sites on the estate and there they remain until they are thought to be able to forage and roost for themselves.

About fifty years ago the method was completely different. Broody hens were bought from local farmers and sitting boxes were constructed by the carpenter and placed in shady positions, usually upon a bank of soil about two feet high, in order to drain any rainwater away that might drown them. Some eighteen pheasant eggs were placed under each hen. Outside each sitting box was a peg with a cord attached and every morning the keeper would tether the hen for about half an hour in order for her to be able to eat and drink, otherwise the hens sat on their eggs day and night for twenty-four days. After hatching, the hen and her pheasant chicks were moved to a coop in the rearing field, where the trouble began.

Boughs were cut from trees and spread on the ground as cover for the chicks who it was hoped, would creep about under the boughs unseen by jack-daws, rooks and hawks. But foxes, owls, stoats and weasels were also predators who liked to eat young chicks so whilst they were so vulnerable, the keepers were on twenty-four hour duty, poor souls. As a rule the chicks would stay with their hen for about six weeks, then they were moved into the woods and left to forage for themselves. These last moves would take place at first light so that the whole operation would be finished before 9 am. It was hoped that the chicks would have found their way around before the night predators began to hunt.

In the old days young pheasant chicks were first fed on chopped hard-boiled eggs. They were then gradually introduced to a mixture of wheat, maize, linseed, hemp and rice, all boiled together in a vast iron vat. Barley and oatmeal were later added for protein and this rich mixture was fed to the birds out in the field four times a day, believe it or not, with cabbage and chopped carrots thrown in, because it was considered that these little creatures loved the vegetables and of course carrots are full of sugar as everybody knows.

When the keeper wasn't chopping up hard-boiled eggs, boiling mash, tethering broody hens or carrying food to the various rearing pens, he was out controlling predators. And when he wasn't setting traps, shooting or ferreting, he was rearing partridge. They were more delicate and difficult to rear than pheasants and round about the middle of September, those which had been reared with such care, would disappear. One fine day, the keeper had been feeding them, everything was seemingly in order, but all to no avail: they had disappeared. One year I became so incensed that I tabbed some of them and discovered that they had fled fifteen miles to an adjoining estate.

The English partridge is, I think a delicious bird to eat and a joy and a pleasure to everybody who has the privilege of being able to shoot. In 1898, which was the year I was born, my father shot over twelve hundred but already by 1918 his bag had dropped to five hundred and by now they are almost extinct. This great reduction in the number of English partridge is the result of changed agricultural methods. Quite rightly, the modern farmer grows the largest amount of crops that he can harvest so he uses every inch of ground and controls weeds with chemical sprays as that gives him the best hope of obtaining the finest crops. However, it does mean fewer nesting grounds for the partridge and less opportunity for them to find the food which they need for themselves and their offspring.

Some people replace the fast disappearing grey-legged English bird with a red-legged breed, commonly known as the French partridge but they usually only fly once, after which, the blasted things run into the hedgerows and sit tight.

I advocate to people, young and old, destroy the French and encourage the wild English by every means in your power. My dear friend Humphrey de Trafford had a lovely shoot at Newsells but I told him, 'Destroy every egg, every nest of the French partridge, as a sporting bird it's a non-starter and it's ruining your shoot.'

His keeper, Gray, completely agreed with me but Humphrey wouldn't listen, with the result that gradually the quality of the shooting at Newsells declined.

Realizing how important it is to make the shooting at Highclere enjoyable for my guests, I go around forty-eight hours before each day's sport, with my head keeper and the beat keeper. I check every drive that they suggest doing, some I agree to and some I change. Then, very carefully, I decide where each of my guests will stand. To my way of thinking, drawing for places is a lazy method. Knowing my ground as well as I do, I place my guests so that at least once during the day each will have a good stand. I have cards made out with the name of each guest showing that he will stand at Peg 2 in the first drive and at the second drive Peg 5, or whatever it may be. He sees the pegs, he can't go wrong. I am there to show him where they are and I hope that everybody, in due course, will get a good shoot. I suppose it is difficult to adopt my way in a syndicate so they prefer to draw and take their chance of being lucky but I've known days when I have hardly fired my gun as I have been most unlucky in the draw!

If I had to give a prize for the two best-run shoots to which I have been invited in the last fifteen years, I would say Biddick and Blenheim, the reason being that each of the hosts knows his estate well and places his guns and makes arrangements, as I have always done at Highclere, to bring out hot soup and warming cheering drinks. These are handed round with a biscuit and a bit of cheese, some time during the morning.

This assuages the pangs of hunger and is immensely popular not only with the guns, but also with the loaders, pickers-up, wives, girlfriends and all who make up the party. The same applies to grouse shooting where, if the weather is hot, iced drinks – I am not talking of spirits, but of cider, beer and soft drinks, and peaches with other fresh fruits are greatly appreciated by the happy band on the moors.

When I was a young man, competition was keen between estates to find out which of them could fill the biggest bag, not who could show the highest birds that could give the best sport. Far from it. My father's keeper would call up the head keeper at The Grange, Alresford, where Frank Ashburton was shooting, and find out what the bag was, and he would then gleefully inform his boss that we, at Highclere, on the same day, with similar weather conditions, had killed more pheasants than they had at The Grange. That news gave great pleasure to my parent and his guests and everybody concerned enjoyed their dinner far more having heard the result of their day's exertions. I am not in the least interested in my neighbour's bags. I am keen on seeing that the pheasants which I have reared fly high and are difficult to shoot so that when people come in they say they have never had a better day anywhere. When I had a syndicate, one of my pals, Cardy Montagu, who was a member, said to me, 'When this syndicate comes to an end, I shall always be able to feel that shooting pheasants at Highclere is, I hope, exactly the same as shooting high pheasants in Paradise.'

I'm sure the following will interest everybody because,
to my mind, it is unique. I have never seen such a thing
happen before. I have a pair of Canadian geese who are
in a field at the present moment, not more than one
hundred and fifty yards from a road which runs right
through the park. Here they have built, in the fork of a
cedar tree, a large nest where the goose sits happily, but
with a beady eye on anybody who gets near her, presumably on four or five eggs, which is about what they
usually lay. Not only does she chase away any cows
that may become inquisitive, she has a good go at any
human being who might be unwary enough to
approach the nest. Photographers have become very
apprehensive of the treatment they may receive from
this cunning old goose. I shall be interested to see
whether the goslings, in due course, reach the ground
safely and I suppose that if they do, their mum will lead
them to a pond, by the name of Redpools, which is
about half a mile away and having reached the water,
presumably they will be able to fend for themselves.

Years ago stoats, weasels, rats and foxes were caught
in gin traps but nowadays these are banned. Birds of
prey, such as sparrow hawks, kestrels, crows and mag-
pies, jackdaws and owls were controlled by shooting
and trapping but the majority of these birds are today
protected by law.

I am a great believer in law and order and in protect-
ing and preserving everything that we can that apper-
tains to the good of the countryside but it does sadden
me to think that the fox, an utterly useless animal is
protected. In hunting countries a moderate amount of
foxes, yes, in order to ensure good hunting to the
thousands who enjoy it. Never in non-hunting

country should foxes be allowed to survive. They are a danger to all and sundry and I beg you to believe me.

Harry Rosebery was Master of the Whaddon Chase and I enjoyed following him to hounds, a very heavy man and utterly fearless, he was one of my dearest friends. He often said to me, 'The more foxes, the less hunting you will enjoy.' In other words, too many foxes will divert hounds in different directions. Foxes do great harm, they are a menace to all game and poultry as they kill for sheer mischief and they carry disease. I live in non-hunting country, except for the Craven hounds which were known in the old days as 'Craven by name and craven by nature', and are now amalgamated with the Vine, so I feel that foxes around here should be destroyed.

If ever the scourge of rabies should come to this country, which God forbid, we would all be in mortal peril and these cursed foxes, which are doing no good, would be the culprits. Nowadays they have become so tame that they go into towns to feed off refuse in dustbins: they breed with ease and there are no restrictions on them, which to me seems to be a very great mistake.

Hunting I have always enjoyed, shooting is one of my greatest pleasures still, but fishing – well, I've only tried my hand at it but once.

I was staying in Scotland with Bertie Ancaster when he suggested that I might try to catch my first salmon. I had visions of landing a magnificent gleaming silver object of immense size onto a grassy bank. My good friend Cardy Montagu, was another guest and we set out together for my first attempt at hooking a fine fish.

I was to be looked after and instructed by the water ghillie who placed me on the river bank some three to four hundred yards away from Cardy who was upstream.

I made several abortive casts then gave a shout of joy as I pulled a little fish out of the water.

'You've hooked a wee salmlet and I'm going to throw him back in again,' said the ghillie and before I could open my mouth to object, he had done just that.

13
Turf Titbits

MY FATHER WAS always interested in racing and it was he who started the stud farm at Highclere. He was an assiduous steward at race meetings and once when he was acting as senior steward at Salisbury, the other two were Billy Bass and Joe Whitburn, a jockey called Scourse, riding a plater trained by Powney, stood up in his stirrups in front of the stand and finished second. Nobody was surprised when the stewards sent for him immediately after the race.

My father opened the proceedings by saying, 'Look here, Scourse, you could have won by about three lengths had you been trying.'

Scourse replied, 'Pardon me, m'lord, not by more than a neck!'

With a stud farm on the home premises, I was drilled in racing lore and management from my earliest years, and have owned racehorses in unbroken sequence since I was fifteen years of age. The first filly I ever owned was given to me by an old friend of my father's, the Vicomte de Fontarce, which I named Virgin Venture, she being by my father's stallion Valens out of Sister of Mercy by Earla Mor out of Vincula.

Some time later I had a very small colt which I

gelded called Linen. He was by Volta out of Cambric. This gelding was trained by Major William Vandeleur Beatty, younger brother of the Admiral, David Beatty.

I happened to be staying with 'Vandy' Beatty, who was a very ill-tempered man. I was devoted to his charming wife, Sybil, and I am happy to say she is still hale and hearty and has remained one of my dearest friends.

On this occasion, curious to relate, she had been locked in her bedroom by her husband who had taken the key with him when he went out with his first lot. David Westmorland's father, Burghie, was also a guest at Phantom House. When we discovered that Sybil was locked in her room, we got hold of a ladder and I climbed up, knocked on the window which Sybil opened and I helped her down. When Vandy returned and found the three of us having breakfast he looked so surprised that we all burst out laughing.

To return to Linen. I had engaged Carslake to ride him in a Selling Race at Gatwick and my dear friend, Monica Sheriffe, said to me, 'I shall not be able to go racing next week at Gatwick, but I do want to know if you think Linen will win.'

'I hope he will,' I replied.

'In that case,' she said, 'I'll have £50 on him.'

Before racing, Vandy said he hoped I'd buy the horse in as he would hate to lose him. I told him I had not the slightest intention of buying him in. Vandy's face fell a mile. Knowing how his mind was working, I thought I'd make sure there was no nonsense, and when Carslake appeared and said, 'Can I have a tenner with you?' My answer was, 'You can have eighty pounds to nothing. Jockeys are not allowed to bet as you well know, but I expect you to win easily.'

Linen duly won. I had taken 700/100 from Joe Bayliss who trained a few horses with Vandy. My trainer had little money of his own and lost the horse after the auction.

There is a sequel to this tale. I was shooting grouse in August that year and before leaving for the moor, I was looking at *Sporting Life* and noticed that Linen was running in the Friary Nursery at Derby. I wired a bet of £50 on him and when I returned from shooting that evening, I learned he had won easily at 8 to 1 against. No betting taxes existed in those halcyon days and the punters had a slight chance of occasionally having a tiny tickle with their 'enemies' in the ring.

When I took over my father's stud at Highclere, I expanded it considerably and built it up into a much larger concern. Here I kept my stallions and a great many brood mares with their foals at foot. I did not train my own horses; instead I would send them to be trained by Dick Dawson, Fred Darling, Harry Cottrill and later 'Atty' Corbett and others.

I had a horse called Tuxedo and he was entered to run in the Manchester Cup. I thought he had a very good chance of winning, as indeed he did, so I decided to watch his performance for myself.

When I got into the train in London, as I was told it would probably be rather crowded, I put my despatch case on the seat next to me. All went well until just before the train started when a huge Mancunian came along, popped his head into the window and said, 'Is that seat taken?'

To which I replied, 'It has a bag on it.'

At this, the man entered the compartment, lifted my bag, put it on the luggage rack and said in a stentorian voice, 'It's bums, not bags, takes seats for Manchester.'

Whilst watching one of the races that day, I was standing talking to Gerald Deane, who had been in the 11th Hussars and was at that time Somerville Tattersalls' partner. Sybil Hare came over to gossip with us both and Gerald turned to her and said, 'Sybil, why are you always called The Electric Hare?'

Like a shot she replied, 'Because all you dirty dogs are always running after me.'

As well as owning horses, I rode for many years as an amateur. When I was stationed at the Cavalry Barracks in York I rode in several races in the north of England and when I could arrange leave, I would also travel to other parts of the country as well. I was mad keen to ride in 'Bumpers' races, as all these events are called by the racing fraternity.

On one occasion, the well-known bookmaker, Issy Isaacs – first cousin of Sir Rufus Isaacs, then Viceroy of India with the title of Lord Reading – asked me to ride his horse Plum at Lewes. I agreed to do so and finished third. As the owner had backed his horse each way at long odds, he sent one hundred of his choicest Havana cigars addressed to me at Highclere. My father's butler, Henry Streatfield, a well-known character with mutton-chop whiskers, opened the parcel and showed my father the cigars which came with Mr Isaacs' compliments and thanks. My father flew into a rage and told Streatfield they were to be returned immediately to the donor. Papa considered it to be gross impertinence that his son, an amateur, should be offered any present.

Issy had a stentorian voice and it was well known that if he thought the favourite was beaten, he would shout, 'The favourite's f————d for fifty.'

Lady Meux was so amused that she told King George v who was her great friend. His Majesty said, 'I must get Porchey to take me near enough to hear him.' The sequel being that one day on returning from riding work at Newmarket, I met His Majesty with one of his equerries. Removing my cap, I stopped to have a word with the King.

'My dear Porchey,' he said, 'I would like you to take me near enough to the rails to hear the bookmaker who shouts "the favourite's f————d for fifty".'

I replied that I would be only too happy to escort him and we arranged to meet a few minutes prior to the three o'clock race. In order to ensure that nothing would go wrong, I told Issy of the little plot.

'You would pick a race of that description', he said. 'A blasted six furlong handicap with heaven knows how many horses running.'

Everything went as planned and as the King returned to his place in the Jockey Club Stand, chuckling delightedly, his parting remark to me was, 'Thank goodness Mildred told me to contact you. My grateful thanks.'

Another tale concerns my adventures on the way to ride at Ayr and the reactions of a professional backer,

Ben Warner, who was going to Ayr believing that the horse which I was to ride, Lights o' London, would win. I agreed and recommended him to have a good bet.

Before going to Euston Station I called in at the Embassy Club in Bond Street knowing I had a couple of hours to put in before boarding the train which was leaving about midnight. I saw a party of friends who invited me to join them and shortly afterwards I was dancing with a lovely lady who shall be nameless. After we had danced together a few times, she said, 'I want to get out of this place. I'll go first and get my coat. You follow me out, we'll get a taxi and go to the station.'

I was more than delighted and the girl and I departed for Euston. The attendant showed me to the sleeping car which had been reserved for me and shortly after I had locked the door we were in each other's arms.

On arrival at Ayr race-course, I found that Lights o' London was in good shape, in fact, in far better condition than his owner-rider. He was a horse with a brilliant turn of foot which lasted for about two hundred yards and, consequently, he had to be covered up during the race and only produced in the last furlong when he would take the lead and win.

On this occasion, I had the mortifying experience of finding, on turning into the straight which is nearly half a mile from the winning post, the leaders swung wide from the rails and my mount, seeing daylight, dashed through it and took the lead. In the last fifty yards, John Nunburnholme, riding a nag carrying bottom weight, beat my horse by half a length. I know it was his first winning ride and probably his last.

I lost my cash and dear old Ben Warner was furious with me: 'What on earth's the matter with you? Are you bloody well crazy? You look like the wrath of God and I expect you were up to no good last night which accounted for your riding such an awful race.'

I told him that he was perfectly correct and that I was ashamed of my incompetence. Poor man, he had lost his bet and most certainly did not deserve to have done so.

A good friend of mine had a spate of losers. He ran into a friend in White's who told him how sorry he was that he was having such bad luck.

The noble lord replied, 'I've thought for years you were a bloody fool and now I'm sure of it. How the hell can anybody be called unlucky who has £65,000 a year to spend?'

I think this tale is a reminder to us all not to moan. What really matters is to enjoy good health and good friends. In both these respects I have been luckier than I deserve. By a great piece of good fortune I was also born slender of frame and light of bone so that it was not too difficult for me to ride to a certain weight. However this did sometimes have its problems. On one occasion I was warned in advance of the difficulty by a nice little lightweight jockey called Joe Plant, who was always known by the nickname of 'Policeman Plant'.

He told me that he had been engaged to ride an outsider which the trainer told him had a good chance. It had bottom weight in the Manchester November

Handicap. He spent a lot of time getting down to the minimum riding weight of six stone and as he felt appalling, his valet said to him, 'I tell you what, Joe, I'll bring you a nice glass of port now you've weighed out and you'll feel ever so much better.'

Joe duly consumed the glass of port and, just for interest, popped onto the trial scales in the jockeys' dressing-room and found, to his horror, that one glass of port had put on seven pounds.

Some time later I had a similar experience. My dear friend Harry Rosebery asked me to ride a horse of his at Windsor, which had ten stone seven to carry. I had a room at the Hammam at the time, so I spent most of the morning getting off all the overweight so that I could weigh out at ten stone seven, on a pound and a half saddle, which I duly accomplished.

Humphrey de Trafford, who was a steward at Windsor, came to see me in the jockeys' dressing-room prior to the race.

'Porchey', he said, 'you look ghastly! I'm going to get you a glass of champagne – you'll ride a much better race.'

I was delighted and after drinking the champagne I did indeed feel much better. However, remembering Joe Plant's tale, I popped on the trial scales and found my weight had gone up by four pounds.

This story is a warning to all weight watchers!

Those who have read *No Regrets* will remember that I very nearly became the owner of a horse called Bland-ford. Dick Dawson, my trainer, bought this yearling colt for me but was persuaded by his elder brother to keep it for himself. Had I owned this great stallion I would have had considerable financial gain and my place in turf history would have been assured. Regrets are vain, but I do regret not having owned Blandford. I also regret not having bought Nearco. I saw him win the Grand Prix in Paris and his owner, Tesio, told me the horse was for sale. Tesio was a great friend and perhaps the most brilliant breeder of thoroughbreds in the world. He invited bids from anyone interested and on the Sunday at the races, I asked him to give me until midday on Monday to arrange finance. I phoned my agent and asked him to instruct Lloyds Bank first thing on Monday morning to have credit made available to me immediately in the sum of £50,000. Next day I offered Tesio £50,000 for the horse. However, he said that in fairness to everybody, bids were being accepted until Wednesday at noon. I waited anxiously to hear the outcome and was very disappointed when Tesio phoned on Wednesday with the news that Martin Benson, a Jewish bookmaker whose real name was Goschalk and who traded under the name of Douglas Stuart, had offered £60,000 which Tesio accepted. He told me that this figure was a record for any horse he had bred. So Nearco went to Beech House Stud at Newmarket and sired six classic winners, of whom Nasrullah was probably the best known.

Nearco, Nasrullah, Blandford and Blenheim were all great horses in their day but I consider that the best I have ever seen in my long life was The Tetrarch, whom I first saw run at Sandown in the National Breeders Produce Stakes when I was a boy of fifteen. After being virtually left at the post, the crowd was thrilled by the electrifying speed of 'the Spotted Wonder' as he was called, brilliantly ridden by Steve Donoghue who got him up and won by a head. When he retired to stud, he sired Tetratema whom I was to see win the Two Thousand Guineas at Newmarket.

Hyperion, owned by Eddy Derby, grandfather of the present John Derby, was a lovely little chestnut horse and the day he won the Derby, ridden by Tommy Weston, is etched in my memory. Tommy, I am delighted to say, is still with us although he has put on a great deal of weight since his days as a top-class jockey.

I am lucky to have a mare by Hornbeam, a son of Hyperion, by name Doushiska who in her turn has proved a successful brood mare and is the dam of Serge Lifar amongst others. I have recently refused a large offer for Serge Lifar from a well-known bloodstock agency, as my able trainer thinks he will prove a far better three-year-old than his exploits would suggest.

To complete the list of those racehorses that I consider to have been outstanding – and they are numerous – I must include the mare Mumtaz Mahal, a daughter of The Tetrarch. She was beautiful to behold and her speed was phenomenal over five and six furlongs, which appeared to me to be the limit of her tether.

All of us who own and breed horses hope that one day one of ours will become famous, and somewhat surprisingly it appears that this desire to own a great racehorse is a very strong one which has overtaken many people in a wide variety of walks of life: writers, politicians, financiers, journalists, impresarios and tycoons often become closely involved in the sport of kings. That most excellent explorer of the criminal mind, Edgar Wallace had a horse running at 'Ally Pally' and I remember talking to him that day when a friend of his accosted him: 'Excuse me, old boy, I hope you don't mind my asking – is that horse you are running in the next race trying?'

Like a flash came his reply, 'By far the most "trying" horse I've ever owned!'

The turf has produced some great individualists and some powerful eccentrics: it attracts those who are larger than life. Dorothy Paget was one of the more unusual figures to be seen at both pre- and post-war meetings. She was said to have an allergy to men. When travelling by train, she had a compartment reserved for her secretary and herself as she could not abide the smell of men. She was enormously rich and her father, Almeric Paget, who became Lord Queenborough – a crashing bore – was also Olive Bailey's father.

I saw Dorothy at race meetings deep in conversation with Fred Darling. There were no women trainers in those days so whether she loathed men or not, she had to have a man to train her horses. Fred found her very difficult to deal with, not least because she was a night-bird. She would telephone him in the small hours to discuss her horses. Finally he had had enough of being woken night after night and was very firm. He said, 'Never call me after 6 pm'. He thought she'd take her horses elsewhere but she didn't. I think Fred Darling was the only man who ever got the better of her.

The turf has also attracted prime ministers. Lord Rosebery and Winston Churchill both owned racehorses and one who had a great affection for them was Herbert Asquith. With his pink cherubic face and beautiful white hair, he was a patrician figure: he and I got on very well together. He loved walking round Dick Dawson's stables at Whatcombe and as Dick had taken over the training of the Aga Khan's horses, he had plenty of very high-class bloodstock under his care. Asquith came quite regularly, perhaps twice a year.

Waldorf Astor was another delightful person who enjoyed horses. One of the nicest of human beings, he took everything very equably, and was a good friend of mine. He bred many good fillies, winning the Oaks at least twice and I found him to be the epitome of an English gentleman. His wife, Nancy, was a bit acid inasmuch as I have known her take up some trivial matter and push it very hard. One of her guests might have unwittingly exposed himself to her criticism and she would give him a good ticking off, which made him feel a worm. As I knew her, I was very careful never to lay myself open to anything over which she could slap me down.

Waldorf was a great supporter of racing in Britain. His horses were trained by that wizard Alec Taylor, a wonderful man and a past master of his art. Astor bred many good horses, but I myself thought that he had one misfortune: his stud farm, which was near his home at Cliveden in Buckinghamshire, consisted of very flat paddocks on clay soil. Nine times out of ten young bloodstock do best when they are reared on limestone soil, which strengthens the bone and lets them develop normally. There is an additional advantage if they are reared in paddocks which are up hill and down dale like my stud at Highclere for they learn when they are foals to open their shoulders and adapt themselves to all types of race-courses. Epsom starts uphill and then has a long run downhill to Tattenham Corner. To succeed here a horse needs to be able to negotiate the hazards of the ups and downs of the course, and to be able to stretch out on any surface for the Derby is run in June, when the ground is usually hard, although these days the going is greatly improved by artificial watering.

I learned at an early age that, if you are going to be a successful breeder of bloodstock, you must start by having in your mind an idea of the type of mare you hope to own. I wished to breed a mare which I hoped would, with luck, produce a medium-sized animal able to negotiate the gradients on all tracks. I always stuck to the principle that nine times out of ten if you had a mare who was capable of winning up to seven furlongs only, then it was best to put her to a horse who himself was top class up to a mile. Instead of putting like to like, many people try to get a blend by putting a sprinting mare to a staying horse. (By a staying horse I mean one who has been proved to win over a mile and a half.) That I consider to be a great mistake. If I have a mile-and-a-half mare, I mate her, if possible, with a good mile-and-a-quarter horse.

The luckiest purchase I ever made – and I've made a great many both good and bad – and the one which gives me perhaps the greatest pleasure in retrospect, is a horse which I bought as a yearling on the advice of my old friend 'Atty' Corbett. In due course I sent him into training, at Compton with Atty, having named him Queen's Hussar.

He is now, I am happy to say, in flourishing health at
the age of nineteen, still very virile and already the sire
of two classic winners: Brigadier Gerard, that great
horse who was only once beaten in his life, in twenty-
seven starts; and another who won the One Thousand
Guineas for Her Majesty, which she named Highclere,
a very delicate compliment which I feel proud to
believe reflected her interest in the Highclere Stud.
This filly, trained by Dick Hern, also won the Prix de
Diane. I was present at Chantilly on the day that the
filly won and Her Majesty got a reception such as you
could not believe unless you saw it yourself. She was
cheered, mobbed and looked very pleased. I burst into
tears. She did not see me do that because I kept well out
of the way and then got into my motor and returned to
Paris.

Since then, Queen's Hussar has bred a lot of good
horses and his progeny have won well over £1,000,000
in stakes.

Curiously enough, although I would not say that
the mares he covered two years ago were in any
way exceptional, I have seen three or four yearlings
by him this year which appear to me to be the best
looking of his progeny. I only pray that the own sister
to Highclere whose name is Blaze of Glory emulates
her elder sister to throw yet more lustre upon Her
Majesty's silks. Nothing could be more popular with
the British public than to see their Queen's successes on
the race-course and I hope she continues for many
years to enjoy this rightly called sport of kings. It has
been said, with great truth, that on the turf and under it,
all men are equal.

Before I finish talking about Queen's Hussar I think

it may interest my readers to know that my son, Lord Porchester, the Queen's racing manager, has contributed greatly to her successes with the wisdom of his judgement.

I suggested that he might like to come over to Compton in Berkshire and see a trial which was taking place early one morning in which Queen's Hussar was going to work with another filly of mine that Corbett thought a great deal of called Anne Boleyn who was by Tudor Minstrel, a couple of other two-year-olds and one good three-year-old. They were going to come five furlongs up the gallops at Compton. When my son saw Queen's Hussar win comfortably by about two lengths with Anne Boleyn second, he was very impressed and, unbeknown to me, when he got home he rang up the breeder of Queen's Hussar who lived nearby and suggested to him that he, Porchester, would like to purchase Jojo, the mother of Queen's Hussar. She was a grey mare by Vilmorin and she had been named Jojo because Joe Childs was the breeder of this mare. Joe was a jockey who had ridden many winners for a number of the leading owners and a very nice man to boot.

Now, what was so interesting was this. The owner of Jojo said, 'Lord Porchester, my daughter is getting married in a week's time and as a wedding present she has asked me to give her a motor car which is costing me £2,200. So, if you give me £2,200, I shall then be able to pay for my daughter's wedding present and you will own the mare.'

Porchester said, 'That's a deal,' and from that moment onwards Porchester has had tremendous success as a breeder because Jojo, carefully mated with

top-class horses, has bred innumerable winners of high
quality and I hope from now on his fortunes will
continue to flourish as a result of this clever dealing.

If you look at Stubbs's paintings of horses racing you
will see that all the jockeys are leaning back with long
leathers. At the turn of the century the first American
jockeys arrived in Europe and their forward, crouch-
ing seat with its low wind resistance was seen to be
very successful. It was adopted by all jockeys from
then on all over the world. Steve Cauthen is not therefore the first American jockey to come over here; many
of his compatriots have been before him. I admire his
strong hands and calm skill. He is, moreover, adept at
changing his whip hand at lightning speed, something
I never mastered.

American influence can also be seen in our horses.
The impact made by horses of American origin all over
Europe is quite extraordinary. Rich men now go to the
USA and buy up the best bloodstock they can lay their
hands on for enormous sums of money.

I was probably indirectly responsible for this craze
for American bloodstock. In 1938 I decided that I
would go and buy a few cheap yearlings at the Saratoga
Sales and when I told Cardy Montagu and Jimmy
Rank what I was about to do, they asked me to let them
come in on the project. Edward Coussell of the British
Bloodstock Agency, accompanied me, as he had frequently attended auctions in the USA and knew the
ropes infinitely better than I did. We spent hours studying the catalogue while travelling over in the *Queen*

Mary. I decided that some of the cheaper looking lots were ideal for my purpose. Cardy had suggested that he and I together should purchase eight yearlings to be landed at Southampton for not more than £700 each. The three I bought for Rank cost rather more money and they all won races. Cardy and I had agreed to draw lots, he to have three and I to have five. Maud Gilroy drew the names out of a hat in our presence and I was very lucky because my five all won and I made a net profit of £7,000 on my purchases, not including several very successful wagers which Humphrey de Trafford carried out on my behalf.

By mid-July 1939, I had won nine races with four two-year-olds which I had bought as yearlings in Saratoga the previous year. They were Harlem, El Morocco, Hot Flash and Robert E. Lee.

Altogether 1939 was a good year for me, as my good friend Harry Rosebery was determined that I should have a big bet on his colt Blue Peter with which he thought, quite rightly as events turned out, that he would win the Derby. He told me, moreover, that I must play up my winnings on this horse in the St Leger for which he was going to be prepared.

I was equally certain, although I did not tell him so, that Pharis belonging to Marcel Boussac, would defeat him. I had seen Pharis win in France and he had impressed me as being probably one of the best horses to race anywhere in the world at that time. I put a monkey (£500) on him for the Leger at 6/1 against.

Owing to the outbreak of hostilities in September of that year, the St Leger did not take place as racing was cancelled. I feel sure I would have won £3,000 if the race had been run!

Pharis was subsequently stolen by the Germans and returned to France at the end of the war where he stood at his owner's stud and proved himself to be an excellent stallion.

Racing and breeding is a way of life and I expect I shall continue to the end of my days. All owners of racehorses are masochists at heart and I am a glutton for punishment. I am always so delighted that the sport manages to continue despite inflation even if the great owners of the past, with their strings of horses have now gone for ever, thanks to the Inland Revenue, who do not allow losses to be offset against tax. They say that as they do not tax winnings, this is fair enough. But it has cut down the number of horses an individual can keep. Some trainers require £84 per week from the owner before the horse even leaves the yard. Lesser lights charge a more modest sum. As a result, today some horses are owned by firms and others by friends who share the costs. However, racing still goes on despite the Chancellor of the Exchequer.

Fifty years ago racing was indeed different to what it is today. In those days I would expect to know three-quarters of the people who frequented the members' stand, whether it was Newmarket, Goodwood or anywhere else, but now I hardly recognize anyone. This is probably very good for the sport and has greatly widened the range of enthusiasts, but I do wish that the modern ardent follower who infiltrates the members' enclosures would attire himself more in keeping with the occasion and would try to behave with greater circumspection.

Standing next to me watching the running of the Two Thousand Guineas at Newmarket a couple of years ago, was an enormous man with a cigar in his left hand and an orange in his right. He was spitting out the orange pips and to my annoyance a pip hit me below my right eye.

'My dear man,' I said, 'if you must spit pips, could you kindly be more careful where you aim.'

To which he replied, 'I've as much bloody right on this stand as you have. I've paid my money to come in and you can shove off if you don't like it.'

All aspects of racing interest me, not only owning and breeding horses, watching them perform and studying their special abilities but also such details as the naming of them, which is an art in itself.

Perhaps one of the best-named fillies I can remember was a mare called Crestfallen, by Ocean Wave out of Dolores. I despise the lazy way in which so many people do it today. For instance, if it is a filly by Swing Easy out of Lady Jane, I find they take one part of the stallion's name and one of the dam's and you get Easy Lady or Swinging Jane. I deplore this habit.

My son and I take a great deal of trouble over horses' names and Her Majesty is remarkably clever at this. Practically all of her animals are skilfully named. I feel it comes from her knowledge of history.

I once had a mare called Malva, which happens to be the name of a lily, for she was by Charles O'Malley out of a mare called Wild Arum, which is also a lily. I bred Blenheim who won the Derby, out of Malva by Bland-ford. I named this horse Blenheim for one reason only:

Blandford is the son of the Duke of Marlborough who lives at Blenheim. Now that was a good name. I could go on for ever on this subject for it fascinates me. I know that there are so many racehorses today that it is very difficult to think of a good new name which has not been used before, but I wish owners and breeders would try harder to be more original.

It is also hard today to obtain racing colours which do not belong to someone else and yet which are easily recognizable from a long way off. Lord Derby's racing colours, black with a white cap show up splendidly from afar. I remember seeing them win the Derby with Sansovino and the Oaks with Toboggan – great moments. I would also suggest that when new – and I repeat, when new – Lord Howard de Walden's apricot jacket is another wonderful colour, easy to see in any field. The late Mr Reid-Walker's colours were sea green and you could see them to perfection. He owned a horse called Dinna Forget which won the Jubilee at Kempton Park. Dinna Forget was very heavily backed from about 8/1 to a hot favourite and I believe started at 7/2.

In those days a big punter known as the Jubilee Juggins won a fortune on that afternoon backing this animal, Dinna Forget. Most of it he won from a very nice bookmaker with whom I had many transactions, the late Charlie Hibbert. He was an old-fashioned bookmaker who lived in Nottingham and he used to come to the races by train, and return by train. He got home that night from Kempton, very tired, he had lost a lot of money and was in no mood for any small talk. His wife said to him, 'Charlie, before you have your supper, I do want you to see the way I've done up the drawing-room. It's brand new and I want you to come and peep at it. I hope you'll love it. I've done it all up in sea green.'

'Mrs 'Ibbert,' said Charlie, 'bugger sea green!'

Here is a tale which illustrates how the unwary can be taken for a ride.

I met a character called Tim McAuley on the *Queen Mary* returning to England in 1947. While dining with him one evening he told me he had a house in Nassau and suggested that he and I might be able to do some very profitable business out there. One of his ideas was that between us we could buy the race-course in Nassau, Hobby Horse Hall, which was at that time run by the Bethell family. When I asked him what this would cost, he said it would be in the region of £50,000, but that all sorts of concessions would go with it and that we would make money out of the tote and out of a licence to sell drinks on the race-course. All in all, he painted a very rosy picture.

When I asked if he was prepared to go halves, he told me he did not have the means but that he would do most of the work in connection with it as he would be on the spot. The most he could afford would be around £10,000, a fifth interest.

I thought the matter over and discussed it with my lawyer. He considered that if I wished to go in for a speculation of this sort, there would be no harm in it. So, we bought the race-course.

Some improvements were needed and one of the first things I did was to have starting stalls built to hold up to twelve animals. Then I arranged for a photo-finish camera to be installed and improvements made to the existing stands.

Another innovation was to segregate the local jockeys in a compound the night before racing, as some of their employers were liable to persuade them not to try. That plan was not popular, as I discovered when I had a visit one day from a well-known Chinaman, who said, 'How do you think we can make a living with all the restrictions you have placed upon us?'

When I asked what he meant, he replied, 'If I think a horse is capable of winning, I don't want any interference from so-and-so and so-and-so, which appear to be the dangers. So, I fix it that those two should not try. Under these conditions, the horse which I back usually wins!'

I told him that my race-course would be run properly and cleanly, and he replied that I would drive a lot of people out of the game and that I would not prosper.

I felt that I should have a clerk of the course and general factotum, so I employed a young ex-trainer, who had held a licence and trained a few horses in Lambourn. I agreed that he should be paid £3,000 a year, which was a considerable sum in 1948.

One of his suggestions was that instead of importing local ponies from the outer islands, we should get Anglo-Irish, or some other agency, to send out about fifty cheap thoroughbreds which we would sell to local people. We got them all landed for about £300 each and we then had a dinner party in the Colonial Hotel to which we invited people who were interested in racing. All the horses were sold to different owners and my friend, Victor Sassoon, bought quite a useful filly which won him several races.

Everything went fairly well and we were quite successful to start with. One day – to my horror – I was told by a local government official that my quota of racing days for the following season was to be cut down to seventeen. One of the reasons given was that the people on the island did not like their servants losing their wages at the races and then asking for an advance.

Matters looked rather gloomy and the following year, 1949, I was told that it would be advisable for me to sell my interests and forsake racing in Nassau. I learned that a certain Mr Alexander Nihon was going to purchase the race-course and racing would continue under his management with the full support of the Bahamas' government.

I consulted my local lawyer and, after protracted proceedings, it was arranged that I should receive £40,000. Ken Goode was paid by me, as he was entitled to be, for the balance of his term of office and the whole venture was wound up.

It turned out to be a horrible ramp because, once I'd been got out of the way, there was a great increase in the number of racing days allotted to the new owner. They were determined to be rid of me so that the whole of the finances should be in the hands of the local patrons of the turf. The only sufferer was silly old me who lost a lot of dough.

Later investigation proved that Tim McAuley had put his fingers into the till on various occasions, helping himself to money which belonged to me. I was present when my lawyers confronted him with his misdemeanours and instead of being put under arrest, he was told that he must not leave the island until all enquiries into the matter had been completed. By the end of that day, he had seen the red light. He got hold of a local motor boat and, at dead of night, sailing without lights, he proceeded to Bimini. The following day he flew from there to the USA, where he went into hiding. In retrospect, I thought it rather peculiar that he had not been ordered to surrender his passport. Eventually he was tracked down and apprehended by an English detective and told that he would be brought to trial in Nassau. Once more he escaped and fled to Canada, where shortly afterwards he ended his days.

I must have been very gullible at that time but I have lived to be considerably wiser in my old age!

I heard a funny story recently about a small-time bookmaker who passed away. When he got to Heaven, St Peter told him he should not be there and sent him to Hell. When he arrived there, he had caviare, oysters, champagne and all manner of good things.

After a few days of this unexpected high living, he met up with a pal and said to him, 'I thought this place, Hell, was meant to be purgatory?'

'It was,' his friend replied, 'but everything's changed here since Ladbroke's took it over.'

14
'Au Revoir'

WHEN I SUCCEEDED on 5 April, 1923, I was told by my trustees and legal advisers that I had not a million to one chance of being able to live at Highclere and that I should build a smaller house in the park and arrange to live modestly.

I replied that Highclere was my heritage and although I knew it would be an onerous task, I was going to do my best to live here. In that I have succeeded.

The late Jack Joel often said to me, 'What you get for nothing in this world is usually worth what you have paid for it.' I hope my faithful friends who have read this book will not feel that they have wasted their money and I trust they will continue to enjoy my television appearances whenever they may take place. I end by saying to those who follow in my footsteps that I hope they enjoy their lives as much as I have enjoyed mine.

Bless you all.

Gold dusted memories of the past
Abide like friends, but falter
Like morning mirages that last
Yet lasting later, alter.

Ah, was that mountain quite so high
And had its flowers that scent?
Could winds be friendly, and as shy
That filled night's starlit tent?

Aubrey Herbert, 1922